BRAUNTON

Tina Gaydon

ISBN 0946 290 20 2

To my husband Stuart in gratitude for his patience,
understanding and endless assistance.

CONTENTS

Grateful thanks to Mary Swailes of the Braunton Museum – without whose help this book would not have been possible. Also the late Lt Cdr J Gammon, MBE, RN, and Mr Kappelman of Kansas. And my mother, the late Grace Incledon and my cousins Peter and Morwenna Incledon. Also all the wonderful Braunton people, but especially Morley Williams, the late John Incledon and Roy Lucas who gave me so much help.

Published by North Devon Books, Bideford
Typeset by Lens Typesetting, Bideford
Printed by Maslands Ltd., Tiverton
1st Published 1989, Revised 2001

CAEN BRIDGE
BRAUNTON. L

Almost every town or village of any importance stands upon a river, and Braunton is no exception. The Caen stream threads its way through the village to join the Taw and Torridge estuary before flowing out into Barnstaple Bay. The village lies north-north east of the estuary, and at the top of West Hill can be seen one of the best panoramic views in the Westcountry. Plainly visible are Saunton Downs and part of Lundy – once the stronghold of pirates and smugglers. Sweeping leftwards along the Bristol Channel the view extends to Hartland Point, and the river Torridge can be seen as it sweeps towards Bideford and it is even possible to see the new bridge with binoculars. Below and to your right is the five

mile stretch of the Braunton Burrows, and to the left the Great Field and the Marshes. As the Taw sweeps towards Barnstaple, the Braunton Pill flows towards you, and on its left bank is RAF Chivenor. Leftwards is Heanton Hill, with its ancient church and cluster of houses. Looking down, the Saunton Road threads its way through the housing estates that have mushroomed down West Hill towards the Saunton Road.

The top of West Hill is called the Beacon and once had a seat which was given to the people of Braunton by the Royal Air Force who flew it there by helicopter. Sadly today all that remains of this seat is two stumps.

This Beacon was used as a signal fire during the days of the Spanish Armada, and in Victorian times the villagers built a huge bonfire there on Guy Fawkes night. It was used again for celebrations at the end of the Second World War, and the coronation of Queen Elizabeth II.

Access to the top of the Beacon is only possible by foot, but is well worth the effort. Older Brauntonians talk with affection of the days in their youth when they did their courting up the Beacon amongst the undergrowth! There is also a very old story remembered by people who played up there before the First World War that the hill was haunted by the old Devil who would be seen staring out to sea.

The best approach is to walk to the end of North Street to the point where it narrows, then turn left at West Hill Lane, and then turn right up into Rock Hill Lane. To your right is the entrance to Frog Lane, and ahead a trackway reaching up amongst the undergrowth to the Beacon. This trackway is marked as a public footpath and is near Berkeley Cottage.

The village of Braunton today is a busy bustling place in the summer when holiday makers throng its shops, and traffic is nose-to-tail as people head for the beaches that run northwards from the estuary. Yet in the winter, Braunton does not become a ghost village, for it is a very popular residential area in which people live yet work in Barnstaple. Its growth over the last thirty years has been rapid for it has almost doubled, and now stands at 10,000. Yet once Braunton was relatively small for in 1801 the population was a mere 1,296.

From its early times when it was a Celtic settlement, Braunton has spread itself along the banks of the Caen stream and has grown up over the hills with residential estates like Saunton Park which in living memory were still fields.

Its growth has been so rapid, that Braunton today claims not only to be one of the oldest villages in North Devon, but also the largest village in England.

Memories of Braunton

There is a quaint old saying that "Braunton was a borough town when Barum was a fuzzy down". Exactly how old no one can say, but I can remember being told as a child that Braunton was much older than Barnstaple.

I have always loved Braunton, partly because I spent my early childhood there, but also because the village has the charm of a place that cares about its appearance. It is rare to find any neglected run-down boarded-up houses that are crying out for improvements. Instead Braunton is a village that is proud of its past, and when progress arrives, it takes advantage of the changes.

An example is the railway. Today all signs that a railway ran through the centre of the village have disappeared, but before Government cutbacks axed the service from Barnstaple to Ilfracombe, the railway dominated the Towns End part of the village. The removal of this railway evoked mixed feelings, for riding aboard the train from Barnstaple to Braunton was very pleasant, especially if the tide was up, and you could see the barges, fully loaded with sand collected from Crow Point, chugging their way up the river Taw.

Today parts of the old railway line have been converted into a walk by the river, which stretches from Barnstaple to Wrafton. It is even possible to make a call at Heanton Court if the exercise proves to be thirsty work! Also there is a seat alongside the fence that skirts RMB Chivenor where it is sometimes possible to catch a glimpse of the helicopters preparing for a mercy mission.

In Braunton itself some of the disused railway line has been grassed over, so it is possible to walk from Towns End to the Fire Station on the corner of West Hill and the Chaloner's Road. The modern fire appliance that is kept ready for action here is a far cry from the old days when the village's fire fighting equipment was a mere hand-cart that was stationed next to Bias Lane in East Street, although the same building was used when motorised vehicles took over the task of fire-fighting.

Where the railway's level crossing once stood there is an anchor set into concrete. Anchors of this size were once dug into the mud around the Pill and used for mooring ships like the *Result*, although this anchor was found by Terry Grace of Barnstaple in the Pill, and belonged to a Jersey vessel called *Mabel*. Braunton Council decided that such an anchor was a fitting symbol for the village with its sea-faring past so they renovated it, and now this area has become a centre where the locals

7

gather to gossip and indulge in unofficial debates, fulfilling the role once served by the old Cross Tree.

When the railway was in operation, and this was a level crossing, I can remember that as children no matter what time we arrived, there always seemed to be a train passing, so the gates would be closed. Despite the lightness of the traffic then, there was often a queue to rival today's snarl-ups in the Exeter and Chaloner Roads.

In Victorian times, when genteel visitors arrived by train at Braunton for a holiday, they would be met by horse-drawn carriages. A house in North Street called "Baroda" was owned by the Clarkes who ran this horse-drawn taxi service. The carriages would wait on the Station's forecourt known as Station Strand (near what is now Squire's Newsagent). Beneath the feet of the horses were platform tiles, and any urine from the animals ran throuh a gully in the tiles straight into the Station Master's garden. He also made free use of their manure, and was renowned for his prize rhubarb!

Today Braunton is an ideal base for holiday makers, for it is within easy reach of the beaches. Saunton is only three miles away, and offers five miles of sand and rolling Atlantic surf. The bathing is comparatively safe provided you go when the tide is coming in, and do not if there is the backwash of a ground sea.

Next along the coastline is Down End, a long stretch of rocks beloved by the locals for hunting lobsters and prawns in its deep pools. The danger with Down End is that it is so easy to become cut off by the tide. Croyde itself is visible from Down End, and is safe for bathing as long as the warning notices are read and believed. The jut of land that lies on the other side of Croyde is called Baggy Point, and around the corner are Putsborough and Woolacombe. During the days of wrecking, Morte Point, which lies further up the coast towards Ilfracombe, was renowned for wreckers who would tie lanterns to the tails of donkeys to confuse the shipping that plied its way towards Bristol. The deeds of these wreckers became so barbarous, and their reputation was so feared, that often sailors realising they were in the grip of the North Devon wreckers, would swim out to sea rather than be brutally murdered.

Nearer to our own time, during the Second World War, fears that North Devon could be invaded were taken very seriously. I can remember seeing gun emplacements at Instow and Saunton. Land mines were laid at Saunton, and as a child I nearly stepped on one, which looked exactly like a saucepan lid, and was only saved by the restraining arm of my cousin. For years these unexploded mines were found, but fortunately in recent times they all appear to have been cleared.

8

The Beacon

Towns End

Old view of the Williams Arms

As it looks today

Staying with the Second World War, an air-raid siren was mounted on the roof of the Parish Hall, and a shelter was built at the back of what is today's car park next to the library. In 1949 the St. John Ambulance made this building their headquarters until 1960 when they moved to Heanton Street into a building once used by the Basket Factory as a store room. Today every Tuesday evening visitors are welcome at their weekly Bingo sessions and the old air raid shelter still stands and is now used by the National Retirement Pension's Association.

Braunton still remembers with pride the part that Rosie Clarke played in the fight for freedom in the Second World War. She was born in 1875, the daughter of "Paddy" Clarke, a rabbit trapper. Rosie was an intelligent girl, and learnt to speak fluent French and German, so she went to work in France as a lady's maid. Later she became a governess, and on her visits to Braunton, was called 'Madam' because everyone thought she was so elegant. Still living in France at the outbreak of the Second World War, Rosie was now an elderly lady of sixty-five, but this did not stop her working with the French Resistance, helping Allied prisoners to escape. For this bravery she was awarded a citation for gallantry.

Braunton itself also was given an award, which can be seen in the gardens leading towards the Caen Field Shopping precinct. It is the Burma Star, and was given to the village to honour the Brauntonians who were in the 'Forgotten army' fighting in Burma. The stone was laid in 1985, and was given to the people of Braunton by The Burma Star Association.

Also the gardens that run alongside the Chaloner's Road bear the name The Memorial Gardens, in honour of the men of the parish who gave their lives in the cause of freedom. These gardens were laid out and given an opening ceremony in the 1950's upon land that had been orchards from the time the Chaloner's Road was built in 1924. Today this garden has a children's play area with swings, and a bowling green. Opposite the Agricultural Inn is a large hedge which hides from view a building which was a slaughter house before the Chaloner's Road was built for it was owned by a Mr Clarke who sold it to a Mr. Ellis in 1920. One day an over zealous lad used too much disinfectant which polluted the Caen stream, much to everyone's disgust. In the days when this building was still a slaughter house, after the Chaloner's road was built, they put a high corrugated fence from today's car park next to the library all the way to Butt's bridge. The slaughter house was still owned by Mr. Ellis, but he sold it to the Council in 1937, who used it as a mortuary. When the Memorial Gardens were made, the building was still being

View of village without the Chaloners or Exeter Roads

used to lay out dead bodies and continued to be so until about twenty-five years ago. There is an amusing story of confusion about these Memorial Gardens because someone took a photograph of them which was then used as a post-card on which they were called Jubilee Gardens, and so people writing about the area assumed this was their correct name.

Returning to the present day, often people who holidayed in North Devon, decided they would like to settle in the area. This population explosion has changed the outlying areas beyond recognition, unlike the old core of Braunton which has retained its shape.

I can remember alterations to the Square. Opposite the George Hotel is the National Westminster Bank. Years ago this building was smaller and was skirted by a low wall upon which, as children, we used to wait for a bus. Today some of this wall still remains around the corner in Heanton Street. There have also been alterations further up this street for it no longer continues on past the junction of Hills View, Wrafton Road and Lower Park Road, but is blocked by a pedestrian walk-way.

The Police Station used to be in Heanton Street, In 1926 it was attended by a Sergeant Summers and one constable. It then moved to the junction of Barton Lane and the Exeter Road, where it remained for many years, whilst today it can be found in the centre of Braunton in the car park.

Before the Second World War there was a garage owned by a Mr Evans on the corner of Caen Street and the Chaloner's Road with petrol pumps. Imagine queuing up for petrol there today!

Many people will remember another shop on the Square, now devoted to surfing, when it was called Flair's. Before the war it was owned by Couper and Woodward and then became Holden's until 1967. Around the corner from this shop in Caen Street were two thatched cottages, which when demolished around the 1930's made way for Slee's and Scoynes which remains to this day.

The Square also had in 1926 a physician and a surgeon called Wright and Traill, who later moved to Towns End. Nearer my own time I can remember an old row of thatched cottages that went from the bottom of Heanton Street towards today's Cross Tree Restaurant. Housed in one of these cottages was Miss Geen's sweet shop next to Howard the Baker. These cottages have all been knocked down to make way for a modern row of shops which continues to the Cross Tree Restaurant, which used to be Atkens the tobacconist. Shops along this part of the Square have seen many changes in the 1950's, for where today is the estate agent next to the restaurant was Tattershell William the dentist, and going towards Heanton Street, Bob Ray's motor cycle shop.

South Street is another area that has altered, and years ago like so much of Braunton it was a street of farms. In living memory two farms survived there owned by the Eastern's and the Palmer's, which today are private houses. In North Street there was Hartnoll's farm which today is Lyndon Close. East Street's farm has been demolished and land has been used for the re-development of a housing estate. At the end of Chapel Street, the part of Score Farm (once called Scure Farm) known as Higher Side, is no longer a farm. Quite recently the Ashton's still kept their cattle, barley, straw and hay there, but along with Palmer's Field, this area is now a housing estate called Ashton Crescent and Palmer Crescent which reaches back to First Field Lane.

Today the only farm which remains in the village is Cross Farm, owned by Mr. Avery on the Saunton Road. Yet years ago when the whole village was full of farm houses, cow pats in the road were a hazard to watch out for, because at milking time all the farmers moved their herds from their grazing lands to their farmsteads inside the village. They all had to cross the Square, and because the herds were so big, and milking times coincided, the herds became mixed up with each other in the Square as they passed. Seven farmers crossed the Square in this way, yet the wrong cow never arrived home with the wrong farmer. It must have been a fantastic sight, the Square full of cows, dogs and shouting men!

In South Street older residents will probably remember the area upon which The Mariners Close Old People's Sheltered Homes now stands next to the pub, and up to Sings Lane. Originally it was the site of the old sawpit, later a carpenter's shop. Up until the 1960's at the corner of Sings Lane was Bert Buckingham's cottage alongside the shed in which he did shoe repairs. Slee's cottage was next, from which he ran a coal business. Next to Slee's cottage was a furniture shop – also owned by the Slee family. Later this building was bought by the basket factory. And how many people can remember the old slaughter house in Sings Lane?

Towards the Square end of South Street, next to Reed's the butchers is a surf shop. Once this was the Liberal Club. Before the Second World War the villagers took a lively interest in politics. Slogans would be plastered on barn doors along with party policies. Meetings were held at the Chaloner's School and in the open air underneath the Cross Tree. The pubs stayed open all day, and free beer was available from both the parties. My mother can remember the whole village turning out to greet the prospective parliamentary candidate to either cheer him on, or heckle him. At the Liberal Club during the days of the sailors, when land-bound by bad weather, they would go there to play skittles or billiards, and during the Second World War it was frequented by so many servicemen that it gained a bad reputation, and became known as "Smokey Joe's".

One of the most famous old photographs of South Street shows the old cottage near the Square with an outside staircase, roughly where today's George Hotel stands. Beside this cottage, up an alley, was a fish and chip shop owned by a Mrs. Smith who would only serve customers who brought their own basin. Staying with this photograph, the building further towards the Square was the old drill hall in which my mother can remember attending dancing lessons, but it also had other functions, for it was used by the forerunners of the Territorial Army, the North Devon Yeomanry, who consisted of farmers and landworkers. After the Exeter Road was built in 1931 a drill hall was built on the left hand side looking towards the recreational grounds at Arlington Terrace, but this building has now been converted into a private house.

Caen Street, which derives its name from the stream which threads its way through the village, is little altered in shape from the time I remember it as a child, only some of the shops have changed hands. The most marked difference is the Cross Tree Shopping Centre, between the Post Office and Lloyds Bank. This shopping centre reaches back with delightfully named Sunny Nook cottages on its left, and a cafe, to emerge from an archway out into the Chaloner's Road. Apparently in the days before betting shops were legalised, a certain gentleman used to conduct a lucrative trade for Braunton's gambling fraternity in one of the old cottages in this area.

The school that stands in Caen Street is little altered, and once was large enough to house all the children of Braunton, from infants to school leavers and when it was built in 1873 it was called the Public Elementary School. In 1937 a Senior School was built at Wrafton Road which later became the Secondary Modern, and is now the Community College. Before 1935 people could pay to send their children to Grammar school but they still had to travel to either Barnstaple or Ilfracombe, but then the State exam came into being as a means of entry to Grammar schools. Today there are both infant and primary schools at Wrafton.

At the end of Caen Street, near Towns End, there is a large free car park. Recently the Braunton Countryside Centre has been opened by the North Devon Environmental Society. This building, on the edge of the car park, offers a wealth of information for all the local events and tourist attractions.

Every year Braunton holds a carnival on Spring Bank Holiday Monday. There is also an amateur operatic society, which recently has staged its productions at Barnstaple. Years ago Braunton possessed a Silver Brass Band and they are often seen in old photographs. They would play to audiences from a pavilion that used to stand at Saunton Park Housing Estate. This band was so successful that they often toured the district giving concerts. Then tragedy struck, for they were aboard a bus which overturned on Stoney Bridge on the Ilfracombe road. The leader, Mr Cockram, was killed and most of the band were so badly injured that they never played together again.

Today the car park spans much of the area that used to house the old railway buildings, and built around its edge is a modern Health and Youth Centre. The building that houses Squire's the newsagents is part of the old railway buildings. I can remember on the Towns End side of the station there was a car park and further up a round building which belonged to W.H. Smiths. Opposite was the surgery of Doctors Wright, Richie and Traill. Then there was the Co-op, Kingdom's fish and chip shop, Hicks and Chugg the green grocer, and the dairy and grocery shop of Poke's. On the Caen Street side of the level crossing was a little wooden gate through which it was possible to walk up the line in the same way one can today, emerging at today's fire station.

Leaving the car park, and going towards Towns End, a modern shopping centre has been built in Caen Field. Years ago, some of the older boys would show off their sporting talent by hitting a ball over its hedge, into the station yard – much to the annoyance of the Station Master.

Saunton Park housing estate was once a cricket and football pitch, where North and South Street boys would sometimes challenge the boys from East and Heanton Street to a football match. This delighted the villagers, for it was always a lively game, because the rules were not kept to if one side found it was losing!

Often today Braunton is viewed as a place which is somewhere that has to be driven through, before reaching the delights of the beach, so people believe what they see from their cars is the true character of Braunton. What these people do not realise, is that the Exeter and Chaloner's Roads are comparatively new additions to the layout of Braunton.

The Chaloner's road was built in 1924 and the Exeter Road in 1931. When the Exeter Road was built so was the George Hotel. The landlord at that time was called George Frankpitts who used to have the Railway Hotel. It is not known if the new pub was called after the king or the landlord! To begin with a wall went from the George right along the Exeter Road and the only shop was Tucker's the newsagent. Later on in the 1930's the locals were particularly impressed by the addition of the Plaza cinema in which they could watch all the modern films, known in those days as 'going to the pictures'. Today this cinema is no more. Later in the 1930's the shops which house concerns like the supermarket were built. Going from the George they were: Ann Gray's dress shop, the Electricity Shop, Richard's cake shop, Mr Banks the grocer, Miss Day's woolshop, a furniture shop and Clarke's the Dairy.

On the opposite side reaching from the bank on the corner was a gas shop, Braund the tent maker, and a hairdresser called Gwenith. Then the same private houses that stand today, and the garage.

Another comparatively new building that is no longer used for its original purpose, is the Methodist Chapel at Hills View, now the Elliott Gallery, which has an Art and Craft Exhibition, and well worth a visit. The graveyard on the Church Street side still remains, but a new Christ Church has been built between East Street and the Chaloner's Road with the amalgamation of the Methodist and the United Reformist.

The oldest part of Braunton is Church Street, where a museum is devoted to local artifacts and photographs, and this building also is a fascinating place to visit for it has a history that stretches back to medieval times and is dealt with in a later chapter.

Local reminiscences from people like my mother often reveal the attitudes of the people of Braunton around the time of the First World War. One that is especially vivid in her mind is of a Mr Moore who was awarded a VC for bravery. In recognition of this award, the village was presented with a gun or cannon, and when Mr Moore stepped off the train he was given a hero's welcome. For years the children played on this gun which was in the field which is now the recreational grounds, until one day it mysteriously disappeared.

Another one of her memories was the cause of a great wonderment to the Brauntonians before the First World War. It was the building of the Braunton Electric Light & Power Company in 1912 on the left-side of the railway line, the Ilfracombe side of the level crossing near the Caen Stream. This company was run by the council, a Mr Clarke and later his son Major Clarke, and an engineer called Welch. Not everyone could have electricity in their homes because it was so expensive, so were the envy of the poorer people. My mother recalls that as children, they walked up the line to stare in disbelief at this new contraption which made the lights in their homes switch on. Then one day the place caught fire, and was so badly damaged that no more electricity was available. Everyone had to revert back to their paraffin lamps as the village was plunged back into Victorian darkness. It was months before the supply was restored, much to everyone's disgust for they had become used to their electricity. After it was repaired the Company continued through to the Second World War.

The shape of East Street has not altered but the shops have. Originally the Post Office started its life at the bottom on the Square, although today the building is little changed. Staying on this side of the street was Daisy Gammon the greengrocer, and Bradly the grocer, and then Bias Lane, and the double doors of the Fire Station. Today it is used by Michael Irwin as a store, but it has been used by the St John's Ambulance who painted the doors black.

On the opposite side of East Street, going from the Square was Dennis the butcher, Williams the tailor, Tossels the shoe shop, Chugg the coal store, a pottery shop, Williams the ironmonger and Ellis the butcher. Then the farm which has now been redeveloped.

Braunton has often been described as a village with one foot in agriculture and one foot in the sea. During its sailing days knowing that there would be sufficient water to make it over the bar was vital, and can be seen by the manner in which the Tide Tables were printed in old Journal Heralds, which said 'Barnstaple Bar. *The following are in Greenwich mean time, but are subject to variations in consequence of the influence of the wind not being taken into account. If local time be required, subtract 17 minutes'.*

Going back even further, beyond living memory, one of the most dramatic impacts on Braunton must have been the arrival of the railway in 1874. With its building, not only could the poorer people travel as they had never been able to do in the past, but exciting new commodities started to appear in the shops, and the farmers found they could sell their surplus products in the cities.

Prior to the arrival of the railway, it was only the sailors who enjoyed the freedom of the 'outside world', and their prosperity was only possible because of the initiative of landowners, who reclaimed the marshland, and straightened the course of the lower reaches of Caen stream.

Although Braunton was isolated before the arrival of the railway, it was always ready to be patriotic in times of war. Braunton men sailed against Napoleon, and so distinguished themselves in the Spanish Armada that the Crown granted Braunton a Charter allowing free moorings for ever to seamen using the Caen stream.

A question often asked is, 'How old is Braunton?' No one can say, but it is believed that Stone Age settlers arrived and lived on the hilltops over three thousand years ago. They probably came by sea, then up the estuary of the Taw and Torridge, for this is the only major inlet along a hundred-mile stretch of coastline from the Camel Estuary in Cornwall, to the River Parrett in Somerset. Known as the Ancient Britons, these were the people who erected standing stones, such as the 'Longstone' at Pilton, Barnstaple.

We know Braunton was originally a Celtic settlement, so it is possible it was inhabited as early as 500 BC. What we do not know is if the Ancient Britons and the Celtic settlers co-existed, and finally merged into a united people.

One interesting historical fact is that the Romans never reached North Devon according to archaeological finds, for apart from a few odd coins nothing remotely Roman has ever been discovered in the area. The Romans did have look-out posts on the coast between Martinhoe and Lynton, but these were possibly only to watch over shipping in the Bristol Channel.

During the thousand years when the Celts lived in the south western peninsula, the area became known as the Kingdom of the Dumnonii, which means the people of the land.

We are sure Celtic people were living in Braunton in 550, because St. Brannock, a Celtic missionary, found people living there and converted them to the Christian faith at a time when the most of England was still heathen.

Another unusual historical event, in comparison to the rest of England, was the arrival of the Saxons. This warlike Germanic race did not reach Devon until 680, centuries after they conquered the rest of Britain. But once they established themselves in the county, they quickly drove out any troublesome Celts, leaving the mark of their domination on the county today, with place names that end with 'ham' or 'tun'. The south western peninsula became known as the Kingdom of Wessex.

It is believed that in Braunton, the Saxons and the Celts co-existed, with the Saxons settling in without bloodshed. This idea is given credibility because the original Celtic dedication of the church still remains.

By 1086, Braunton had grown into a Royal Manor of considerable wealth, and had spread itself along the low-lying banks of the Caen stream, with a massive open Field that still exists today, known as Braunton Great Field.

With the Norman Conquest, the effect on Braunton was to reduce the free landowners into bonded tenants, who were made to work their own land. But this bondage did not last for ever, for as the village developed through the middle ages, to modern times, the Braunton people asserted their spirit of independence, regained their freedom and created the unique village that exists today.

St Brannock

The first thing that you notice when you visit Braunton's parish church is that it is not where you would expect to find it – in the centre of the village, but lies almost outside on its northern boundary.

This apparent break with tradition is deceptive, for in the days when the church was built on this site, it *was* in the centre of the village. At this time the Celtic community was very small, but when the Saxons arrived they concentrated all their development southwards, towards the fertile valley in which they made their Great Field. And later, when the improvements to the Braunton Pill increased the sea-going trade, this southwards sprawl continued for the sailors preferred to make their homes in the fast developing residential area of South Street.

Today's beautiful thirteenth century church stands in a graveyard that is flanked on one side by Chaloners Road, and the ancient Church Street on the other. It is believed to be the third church to have been built on this site, although nothing remains today of the original, or its successor, except a slab of stone which can be seen near the west window.

The story of this church reaches back to the year 550 when, so the local legend tells us, a monk arrived on Saunton Sands called St Brannock. He had floated over the Bristol Channel from Wales aboard a stone coffin. (This 'coffin' could have been a 'lech' or tombstone which all the Celtic saints supposedly carried with them on their pilgrimages.)

In Wales St Brannock had lived in the royal household of Brychan, the King of Brecknock. Although he was a priest, he was also married to one of the King's daughters, but because of family quarrels decided that he would like to leave home.

At this time the Welsh Celts frequently made raids on North Devon, and it is possible that it was on one of these trips that St Brannock suddenly appeared on Saunton Sands, although a third version declares that he rode into Braunton one day on the back of a donkey.

But by whatever method he arrived the people who greeted him were still very pagan, believing in, and worshipping, the nature spirits who were reputed to live in the trees and rivers. At this time the community consisted of isolated farmsteads grouped around Chapel Hill. The Braunton we know today was still virgin forest, or scrubby woodland.

Upon his arrival St Brannock named the place "Brannockstond", and settled down to teach the people more productive farming methods whilst he converted them to the Christian faith. We will never know

how difficult he found it to persuade them to abandon their practises of sacrificing young children in the name of appeasement to their nature spirits, and their other pagan beliefs. But once his flock was converted and everyone became practising Christians, St Brannock turned his attention to building them a church – the first one to be built in North Devon.

Chapel Hill was selected for this historic building. Timber was collected from the nearby forest to be hauled up the hill so they could proceed with the task. The only problem was no matter how long, or how hard everyone laboured, come next morning some unseen force had torn it down during the night.

It is interesting to speculate what the superstitious Celts made of all this, but after a while, in true Christian tradition, St Brannock saw a vision. It was of an angel who told him he should go and seek a meadow in which he would find a gently flowing stream. There he would find a white sow who would be suckling her seven piglets. The saint did as he was instructed, finding the meadow with the stream, complete with the sow and her piglets, just as the angel had predicted. Satisfied that divine intervention was at work they abandoned Chapel Hill and started work on the church where today's building stands.

There has been a great deal of speculation about this particular legend. Like all folklore, there is probably a grain of truth in it somewhere, but the Celtic saints appear to have performed in very similar ways. They were all credited with possessing supernatural powers which the Celtic people would have believed in, for they were that way inclined themselves.

One thing that is worth bearing in mind is that after the Norman conquest there was a renewed interest in the lives of all the native saints. This could have been to increase the feeling of religious fervour in the ordinary people. Every saintly life was investigated and the details were written down. To qualify as a saint a person must have been capable of performing miracles. If no evidence of this could be found, then the writers stole or adapted from existing legend of other 'qualified saints'.

With Braunton there was no need to invent, for St Brannock was an extremely talented holy man. So much so, that by 867 it had become an important religious shrine which held the status of a 'Minster'. We know this because of a reference in a Glastonbury Charter, which tells us that King Ethelbald gave 1,200 acres of land at Brannocksminster to the Abbot of Glastonbury for the 'taking of salmon'.

Some of the events of St Brannock's life could well have been stolen by the Norman writers for other saints, for the story of a church being

The unique carved pews

The old village stocks

mysteriously torn down occurs in other parts of Devon, and even further afield. And there was also a widespread belief that any spot in which you found a sow with her piglets was very lucky, for they were considered to be a protection symbol of the "mother church".

But there are other stories of St Brannock that are unique. He was reputed to have been able to catch, and yoke the deer that roamed the surrounding forest, and this was how the timber was transported to the site of the church. And when he was in Wales he was credited with bringing a cow back to life. She was a great favourite of his, so his enemies killed her and chopped up her body into pieces which they then put into a pot of water to be cooked over a fire. Mysteriously, the water refused to boil, or even become warm, much to the amazement of the onlookers. At this point St Brannock discovered their crime. Taking the pot from the fire, he 'breathed life into her' and miraculously revived her.

Returning to the church on the hill that refused to be built: there could be a very practical reason for this legend. The Celtic people preferred to build their defensive forts on the top of a hill, and although Braunton during this time was not being attacked by the invading Angles, Jutes and Saxons, word might have reached them from their Celtic brethren of the wholesale slaughter that was taking place in the rest of England. So, purely for defensive reasons, they would have wanted their new house of worship to be high up on a hill, rather than the low-lying valley area of the village.

St Brannock may have agreed to this spot with great reluctance, for being a holy man death would hold no terror. He probably considered it far more practical to build the church on the more easily accessible area of Church Street, rather than on top of Chapel Hill. Maybe those unknown forces were not so mysterious after all?

When St Brannock died, his mortal remains were buried at Braunton, where they have remained to this day. It is this fact that makes Braunton so unique, for few churches can claim the distinction of possessing the whole body of their Patron Saint. Usually a dedication would rest on ownership of merely a small relic from a holy person, and later churches would be named after a Roman dedication, as for example St Peter, or the Virgin Mary.

During the reign of Elizabeth I we find that it was not just the complete body that the church owned, but other relics as well. According to tradition, every year on June 26th, these relics were paraded around the streets of Braunton, for this was supposed to have been the date when he was interred beneath the high altar of the church.

An intense religious fervour for Braunton's Patron Saint has survived down the centuries, for when Henry VIII's men came to ransack the church after the Reformation the villagers turned out, from the smallest lad to the oldest citizen, to form a protective ring around their beloved church. Their determination was so fierce that the soldiers gave up, and left the church unmolested.

The present church is Norman, and was built in 1310. It has a lead-covered timber broach spire; one of only three in North Devon, the others being at Barnstaple and Swimbridge. It is possible that the lead was obtained locally, for the Combe Martin mines were still in operation at this time. From the church-warden's accounts kept during the seventeenth and eighteenth centuries, it can be seen that the spire needed constant attention – so much so that they had to make a special ladder to carry out the repairs.

During the Second World War, when work was being carried out on the high altar, a stone coffin was discovered full of bones. The people concerned, being rather squeamish, hurriedly put the lid back, and covered the hole. Was it, one wonders, the mortal remains of St Brannock.

Inside the church, the cradle roof has a number of fascinating bosses, one being of a sow and her family. Another is the heraldic coat of arms of the Gorges family, which is similar to a whirlpool. This family played a major role in the history of Braunton, for they owned one of the chief manors.

But the most striking feature, without equal in Devon, is the remarkable chestnut pews. They are very well preserved, for church records date them as being made between 1500 to 1600. They are divided into four blocks, by a broad central passage from the West Porch to the Chancel Arch, and by a passage that runs from the South to the North Porch.

They are carved, in varying degrees of competence, with the figures of saints and other religious symbols. Some have been defaced, probably during the seventeenth century, others have upside-down initials, thought to have been a sign of humility by the donor, while the ones that are near the altar depict events in St Brannock's life, such as the one that shows him with an ox.

Knowing the legends of Braunton it is fascinating to look at the ends of these benches and make your own interpretation of their meaning. Apart from St Brannock there is, for example, a carving of a ladder. Was this the one made to repair the spire? There is also a castle, perhaps to denote the Norman Conquest? Probably we will never know, but this just makes St Brannock's church so much more interesting.

The parish church is not the only place of worship in Braunton today that is dedicated to St Brannock. From medieval times there was a chapel, named after the saint, which stood beside a well on the wooded slope which overlooks the village of Braunton, just below Buckland House.

By the eighteenth century, this chapel had become nothing more than a ruin with rubbish choking its well. Then, in the 1950's, Mrs Angela Incledon-Webber decided to have a Roman Catholic Church built on the site, dedicated to the saint and this was completed in 1956.

Beside the church door can be seen the foundation stone which was laid by the Bishop of Plymouth. On it can be seen a curious fossilised mollusc that is over 140 million years old. And appropriately, remembering the early Christian's symbol, it is in the shape of a fish.

BRANNOCKS CHURCH, BRAUNTON.

Development of a Village

The early development of Saxon Braunton was based on the principle of the open field system. Once the virgin forest was cleared, the early village was laid out along the lines of an open field known as an 'infield', 'outfields' being the Great Field, and another on the Downs.

These Saxons were less barbarous than their Germanic ancestors who butchered the Celts; partly because these Saxons were the descendants of the original invaders, but also because after three hundred years in Britain, they had become converted to the Christian Faith and this is probably the reason they respected and co-existed with the Braunton Christian Celts. Although, the Saxons were trained warriors intent on the complete conquest of Britain, they were at heart home lovers looking for a place to farm. How they must have looked with wonder and relief at the virgin forest of Braunton, knowing that their fighting days were over, and that they could settle down in this 'Garden of Eden'.

The heart of the Saxon settlement was today's Square, whilst St Brannock's church remained the centre of the Celtic Community. Links between the two races were forged, for East Street ran northwards from the Square to link with ancient Church Street, although at this time these 'streets' would have been mere tracks, rather like the headlands in today's Great Field.

The Saxons erected a massive stone cross in the Square which, it is believed, was used as a preaching post. Usually these stone crosses were replaced by churches, but as this did not take place in Braunton, we can only assume that the co-existence was so peaceful that in time the two races worshipped together in St Brannock's church.

It is believed that this stone cross was removed to the churchyard of St Brannock's church in the seventeenth century, and an elm tree was planted in its place. This tree then assumed the role of being the centre of the social life of the village. It was a place to gossip and generally 'set the world to rights'. By Victorian times four public houses were clustered around this elm tree and ringbolts were driven into its trunk for tethering horses. Public notices were attached to it, children played marbles beneath it, and often were joined by home-coming seamen. The tree was used as a 'soap box' for political meetings, and often drunken protagonists spilled out from the pubs to fight around it when their arguments became overheated. The Volunteers and Yeomanry paraded before the tree on their way to annual summer camp. People of the Gospel Hall would gather beneath it, as did the Salvation Army. The town crier rang his bell under it. And during the summer, the villagers would sing and dance around it. During Victorian times the villagers were dazzled by the wares of the cheap jacks who used it as a shop. Then, in 1935, the old tree was felled leaving the feeling that the village was losing a friend, rather than a tree. Today in a pavement outside of the Cross Tree Restaurant is a plaque in honour of the old tree, but in reality, the tree stood further out in the road.

Returning to the original stone cross, judging from a print of an old engraving which can be found in the museum, it appears to have been very large in comparison to a ninth century example which is on display in the British Museum. It is believed that Braunton's cross was struck by lightening after its removal to the churchyard, and that some of its stone was used in the outside walls of one of the houses in Church Street.

Saxon Braunton became a Minster, so its church was the most important one in North Devon. The village also headed the political system known as the hundred, with authority over places like Ilfracombe and Challacombe.

Being a Royal Manor, Braunton had to pay its dues to the King of Wessex. Often these Saxon kings gave away portions of land, as happened with Braunton, for the king gave the Abbot of Glastonbury 1,200 acres of Braunton in exchange for salmon.

With the Norman invasion came the manorial system in which the villagers were bound to the soil. They were expected to farm their lord's lands, and also keep him supplied with honey, cheese and eggs. When land was sold, the people who worked upon it were also sold. The Braunton villagers, although no longer free, do not appear to have been treated harshly, probably because these early Norman lords were absent landlords who left the administration of Braunton to a Sheriff.

The last invader, or 'immigrant' to arrive in Braunton was the rabbit. The Normans introduced them as a tasty change from the salted meat in the winter months. At first these rabbits were farmed in man-made warrens, but quickly escaped and turned wild, spreading to the sand dunes – which is the reason the Braunton Burrows is so named. These rabbits bred so quickly, and did so much damage to crops, that 'rabbiting' soon became a rewarding pastime.

From Norman times Braunton slipped into isolation, leaving Barnstaple to take over the role of 'capital' of North Devon. This isolation had its advantages, for when the bubonic plague (Black Death) killed a third of the English population, Braunton remained untouched.

Braunton's growth can be traced by its maps, the oldest being dated 1575. It shows 'Cryd' (Croyde), 'Ham' (Georgeham), 'Santon'

Start of the Butts

Cottage and gate in Butts, and the old railway line

The Skir continues

The Butts becomes the Skir

And around the corner widens

(Saunton). In the village can be seen the church, with pathways radiating to the surrounding tenements, which over the years became 'promoted' to the streets of Braunton.

On a later map, dated 1765, some of these paths are clearly defined as streets. Church Street is linked to Sylvester Street (Silver Street) meaning growing in the wood, and today Silver Street still threads its way out to Knowle amongst the trees. Church Street is linked to East Street, and at this junction North Down Road now forks up into the hills to Boode and Ash Road. Returning to the Square, Heanton Street now leads to Lower Park Road and then continues as the 'main road' to Ashford. The Great Field is shown, along with the outfield on the Downs.

Exeter Road and Chaloner's Road along with Caen Street did not exist, but Butts and Bias Lanes are clearly defined. These pathways are of special interest because it was in the Butts Lane that the men practised archery at straw targets. The name 'Butts' has two meanings: one is archery butts; the other is 'a strip of land abutting onto boundaries' and Braunton's Butts qualifies for both meanings, so it is impossible to detect the origin of its name.

To walk the ancient Butts today start in St Brannock's churchyard. From here cross the stream, and you will see the Chaloner's Road. Across this road there is a second pathway, because the Butts became severed when the main road was built. Cross to this, and towards its end, notice the cottages to your right, and a gate in front of you. Once through the gate you are walking on the old railway line. Directly opposite, you will see another gate, and once through it, the Butts becomes the 'Skir'. Again notice the quaint little cottages to your right. As the Skir (meaning to ramble over – or run hastily) turns sharply to the left, at its top it widens out before leading out into North Street. Referring once more to the 1765 map, North Street and Chapel Street were once one long road called West Street. At this time Caen Street, Towns End and the Saunton Road were not 'promoted', and were mere tracks.

So the village at this time was: West Street, running on the west side of the Caen, Silver Street continued on into Wrafton – forming the east of the village. Heanton Street, leading to Lower Park Road ran up over the hills to Ashford, and North Down Road went to Boode and Ash Road (out in the country).

The Butts linked the village from east to west, and the Bias ran from East Street to Caen stream. Like the Butts the Bias was severed when the Chaloner's Road was built. Now it runs from East Street out into the

The Skir runs into North Street

From North Street a fork brings you to West Hill

North Street looking across to Chapel Street

main road, and appears to be merely an alley-way. But once it was flanked by cottages, and older residents can still remember the days when it continued its path across where today's main road severs it, and then turned right before it ran alongside the playing field, ending where the stream makes a loop. It is thought that its original function was to give the villagers access to the Great Field, via the Field Lanes. To gain access to the 'outfield' on the Downs, there were Willow, Frog and Pixie Lanes, leading up from West Street via West Hill Lane.

The next change in Braunton's appearance came between 1765 and 1809 when Caen Street, Towns End and Saunton Lane were at last 'promoted'. Soon Braunton would enter the early Victorian era, when its rate of development brought dramatic changes to the villages. These changes will be told in later chapters, but first we must retrace our steps and examine the manors, the Great Field and the Marshes.

Chapel Street looking back into North Street

The Manors

After the Norman Conquest in 1066, Braunton became divided into the three Manors of Dean, Abbots and Gorges. The affairs of these manors were dealt with at the Manorial Courts in the old Parish Rooms, next to the church. Each Manor elected their own Ale Taster, Pound Keeper, Reeve, Beadle, Constable, Gate Keeper and Town Crier.

The Manor of Dean included St Brannock's church and land as far as Knowle where the Manor house was situated. Today as Church Street curves towards the Chaloner's Road and crosses the Caen, the bridge is still named Dean's Bridge. The Manor of Abbots had land near Heanton and at Fairlinch between West Hill and today's Saunton Road; also out of Braunton on the old Barnstaple Road, at Luscott, was its Manor House, which is today's Park Farm. Today between Hills View and North Down Road is still called Abbots Hill.

The Manor of Gorges owned North Street, and Chapel Street. It also had East Street where its Manor House, called the Hall, known today as Broadgate, still stands. This old house gives us an insight into those days of grandeur because it is such a beautiful old house. It still retains most of the medieval timbers in the roof, and has outbuildings which flank East Street, The garden faces the main road, and before the Chaloner's Road was built reached right down to the Caen stream.

The Manors of Abbots and Gorges also owned land in the Great Field, the Downs, and the Marshes, all of which was farmed by their tenant farmers. By Victorian times more and more of these tenants had become owners, and so the manorial system at last ended in Braunton.

Another separate manor which stems from Norman times is Buckland Manor on the northern fringe of Braunton near the pretty Roman Catholic Church, home of the Incledon-Webbers. The Incledon branch of this family was awarded lands at Croyde and Putsborough, along with the foreshore of Croyde, and part of Putsborough, in 1160.

Today's pub by the river at Heanton Court was once a manor house, built during the reign of Heny VIII. This was a separate manor, and the original Norman lord, Richard Punchardon, upon returning from the Crusades in 1290 built the beautiful church dedicated to St Augustine that still stands today, in the parish named after him.

And the respect the people felt for the lords of these manors still stayed until Victorian times, for the Post Office Directory dated 1856 still listed people as either Gentry or Tradesmen.

Entrance to Broadgate in East Street

What is left of Broadgate's garden

The Great Field

The first time that I walked into this famous Great Field, I wondered what all the fuss was about. I knew how special it was, for it is a classic example of the way in which the land was once cultivated in medieval England. In those days most villages were surrounded by such open-fields, but they have, with the exception of one at Laxton in Nottinghamshire, long since disappeared – sacrificed in the name of modern development.

Knowing this, I felt puzzled as I walked deeper into the historic field, for it looked so very ordinary with a hedge on my right and grass beneath my feet. As I had gained access via a gate in the Marsh Road, the land, to begin with, sloped gently upwards, but at the top of this incline, the hedge came to an end, and there before me, the Great Field spread itself. It was enormous! Straight ahead, as far as the eye could see, right up to the gently rolling hills, and, looking to my right, it appeared to nestle right into the very edge of the village.

No camera is capable of capturing the visual impact of the Great Field, for its spaciousness has to be seen to be believed, and no words can express its peacefulness, and sense of antiquity. I would not have been at all surprised to see a Saxon, complete with plough and oxen, working in this ancient field. So now I, too, understood what all the fuss was about. But why was it so flat? (Actually, it is not flat – it's dome-shaped).

It seems that it owes its appearance to the geological changes that were taking place here nearly two million years ago. Then, as each Ice Age either tightened or loosened its grip, the polar ice cap advanced or retreated, making the sea levels rise or fall. This created terraces in the river estuary, upon which the melting ice deposited alluvial silt, clay and peat of up to 120 feet thick. One of these terraces became today's Great Field.

The land that resulted proved to be so good, that a 1640 historian remarked that Braunton was 'a parish so fertile for soil, that it is reported for credit some fields there are never uncultured, bearing barley with great increase.'

But before this historian could make his statement, the Saxons had to arrive in this peaceful valley. At this time, the Braunton Great Field was still thickly wooded, and today, looking at the neatly cultivated strips, their task of chopping and clearing away the trees appears daunting. Yet they achieved it, with only the use of very simple tools, over 350 acres, right up to the point where the terraced shelf met the

Aerial view of the Great Field

Some of the strips have disappeared

But not all of them

marshes. Here, they built a bank for protection against the salt spray when the tide flooded the marshes, and planted a blackthorn hedge on its top that still flourishes there today.

Next, they divided up their acreage into the famous strip system, and they must have been very knowledgeable farmers, for they utilised any slight incline so that they could plough the land in such a way that would encourage good drainage of the soil.

Today a portion of the Saxon division of this Great Field still survives, giving us the opportunity to marvel at their ingenuity. Their method was to apportion a Great Field into blocks of furlongs (220 yards) which ran from a strip of uncultivated land called a headland, upon which they could turn their ploughs without having to trespass on each other's land. Next, they further divided each furlong of land into narrow strips, measuring either 5½ yards (¼ acre) or 11 yards (½ acre) wide by a furlong (220 yards) long. These strips, (or plots or lands) were separated from each other by a mound of earth that was approximately one foot high, and roughly the same width, called a balk, but known locally as "landsherds". These landsherds became grass covered, and were created originally by a ploughed furrow from each side of an adjoining strip, and at their ends, the Saxons placed smooth boulders called "bond stones" to mark this permanent division of their strips of land.

Edward I in 1305 decided that all the strips in such fields as Braunton's should be of one acre each (although Braunton appears to have taken little notice of this 'Royal Command', for the field still retains some of its original Saxon ¼ and ½ acre strips). Edward's idea was the medieval equivalent of the modern-day work's study, for it was decided that a man, with a plough that was pulled by two oxen, could plough one acre in a day.

It was therefore going to be a permanent measure of all the strips in the nation's 'outfields', so you would have (that is, if you took any notice of King Edward) a strip which measured 22 yards by 220 yards, making 4840 square yards, which is one acre.

It is very interesting when you realise that today we are still using this medieval method of measurement, for our mile is still made up from the old, Saxon table of 5½ yards making one pole (the ¼ acre strip), two of these 'poles' and you have the ½ an acre strip, 4 of these 'poles' give you King Edward's acre – or one chain. Ten chains equals a furlong (the length of the strips) and eight furlongs makes one mile. The 5½ yard 'pole' was the length of the wood which the Saxons used to drive their oxen.

To return to the early Saxons. Once their fields were laid out, the method they used to share out their land was that the chief (the thegn) would have at least 500 acres for his own use (well over 1,000 strips of ¼ or ½ acre). The freeman (the ceorl) would have about a hide of land (100 acres) which would be between 100 to 400 strips, depending on their width. This was considered to be the amount of land that was needed to support a man and his family. Both the thegn and the ceorl could pass on their land to their descendants, unlike the poorer people, who rented part of the thegn's strips, for which they were obliged to pay him dues in the form of sheep, chicken, and barley. Also, they were made to work two or three days a week on the remainder of their chief's strips. These people were 'bound to the soil' and could be sold or exchanged with the land that they worked. Below them came the slaves, both field and house, although in the case of Braunton, it is believed that everyone was in the class of the 'freemen'.

But the status of the owner made little difference when it came to the allocation of the land, for everybody's strips were purposely scattered throughout the 'outfields', so every one received an equal share of the marsh, stones or the fertile land.

They also shared the ploughs and oxen. Each family was obliged to supply part of this 'team', so two farmers might supply, say, two animals each, while a third would put the plough. All three would have the right to use this 'team' of plough and oxen, although exactly how they arranged their 'turns' without arguments when the busy season came, is left to our imagination.

We do not know if, originally, the Braunton Saxons followed the pattern of using one field for wheat to make bread, the other for barley to brew beer, with a third left fallow so it would rest, and be used to graze cattle who would obligingly manure it at the same time, for the Great Field was not the only 'outfield' that they possessed. There were two others, one on the Downs, and a smaller one to the north east of the village.

Looking at the Domesday record, it lists the manor of Braunton as possessing thirty ploughs, but with enough land for forty. This suggests that only one quarter was left fallow in any one year, for in addition to the 'outfields' they possessed grazing for their cattle on the Braunton Marsh.

Also, the actual village itself was really an 'infield', in which the dwelling house faced the road (or lane) with ground at the back, which, by Tudor times had become divided into out-buildings, vegetable patches, and orchards, where you would find pigs and poultry. This was because Braunton developed quite unlike the traditional idea of a farmhouse, with its yards, out-houses, cowsheds and orchards, all surrounded by fields that were enclosed into one complete unit of a 'farm', with hedges.

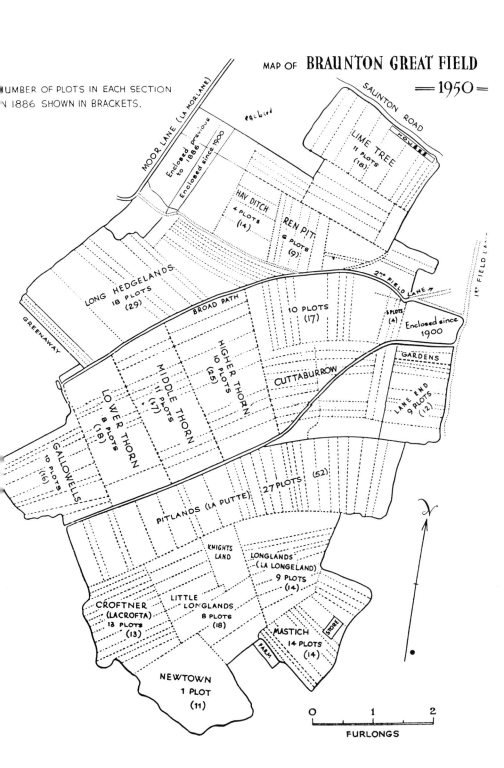

MAP OF **BRAUNTON GREAT FIELD**
═══ 1950 ═══

NUMBER OF PLOTS IN EACH SECTION
IN 1886 SHOWN IN BRACKETS.

MOOR LANE (LA MOR LANE)

egcbird

SAUNTON ROAD

HOWELL

Enclosed previous to 1886
Enclosed since 1900

LIME TREE
11 PLOTS
(18)

HAY DITCH
4 PLOTS
(14)

REN PIT
6 PLOTS
(9)

2ND FIELD LANE

1ST FIELD LANE

LONG HEDGELANDS
18 PLOTS
(29)

BROAD PATH

10 PLOTS
(17)

3 PLOTS
(4)

Enclosed since
1900

GREENAWAY

GARDENS

HIGHER THORN
10 PLOTS
(25)

CUTTABURROW

LANE END
9 PLOTS
(12)

MIDDLE THORN
11 PLOTS
(17)

LOWER THORN
8 PLOTS
(18)

GALLOWELLS
10 PLOTS
(16)

27 PLOTS   (52)

PITLANDS (LA PUTTE)

N

KNIGHTS
LAND

LONGLANDS
(LA LONGELAND)
9 PLOTS
(14)

CROFTNER
(LACROFTA)
13 PLOTS
(13)

LITTLE
LONGLANDS
8 PLOTS
(18)

MASTICH
14 PLOTS
(14)

STORE

FARM

NEWTOWN
1 PLOT
(11)

0   1   2

FURLONGS

With Braunton, the farmer's house was in the town, and was referred to as his 'town house', whilst his 'farm', was in the 'country' of the outfields, that were connected to the village by such romantic sounding names as Pixie, or the unaccountable Frog Lane.

And even after the Normans arrived it remained the same. The parcels of land that were being given away by the King, or, later were sold or exchanged, were still 'in the town' or 'in the country' and were scattered all around the parish.

Some of the ancient rights of the Great Field were still being enjoyed, right up until a hundred years ago. One was that as soon as the harvest was safely gathered in, the field would then revert back to common land, so all the villagers could graze their cattle there, once Barnstaple Fair was over in late September. Old folk and children would go to the field armed with rakes to search for corn ears, which they would gather up into bunches, known locally as 'sangs' which provided a valuable source of winter food for the prized family pig, or the poultry, which was still being kept in the back gardens and orchards of Victorian Braunton. These common rights were called 'leasing' or 'gleaning'.

The practice of keeping a pig in an orchard endured right up until the Second World War, and people who still remember those days will tell you that when it was time to kill it, it had grown into a fearsome 300 lb. animal (three times the size of the pigs that are slaughtered today) and that this huge beast butted the apple trees to make the fruit fall to the ground which they greedily devoured. But once the pig had been killed, its flavour was something that we moderns, with our desire for the leaner cuts can never know anything about – more's the pity!

But to return to the Great Field. As already mentioned, the ownership and common rights of the 'outfields' were intermingled and scattered throughout their acreage. The lands belonging to the Gorges, apart from their 'town holdings' were mostly on the northern part of the Great Field adjoining the Saunton Road, whereas the manors of Dean and Abbots gradually acquired, over the years, large portions of land on the Braunton Down's, and on the north and east of the village, although several of the tenants of the Abbots had strips in the Great Field.

Today there are very real fears that the Great Field will gradually disappear in its ancient form. It is not classed as an ancient monument, so farmers are under no obligation if they want to plough it up in any way they please. With the passing years each owner, upon acquiring land, has made it more suitable for modern cultivation by ploughing up the landsherds and making larger plots. For example in 1950 enough strips were joined together at "Lime Tree" to make a six acre plot.

Typical farm 'Townhouse' but now developed into a housing estate

Mill Style

Similar joining of strips has taken place all over the Great Field and on the Braunton Down.

But Braunton is proud of its Great Field, and today's Parish Council recently made an approach to "English Heritage", in the hope that the field might be given ancient monument status. Once these unique furlongs and headlands are ploughed up, the whole structure, that is the essential skeleton of the field, will be lost forever.

Concern over the conservation of the Great Field is nothing new; historians have always viewed it with interest, and its links with the past are realised when you compare an ancient document dated 1324 in which you will find the same names of Pitlands, Longlands, and Crofner, that can be found on modern ordnance survey maps today.

But there is no doubt of the decrease of the strip system, for in 1889 70% of the strips were still intact, and numbered 491 owned by 56 farmers and tenants. Today, the field is owned by only a handful of farmers, and the strips have shrunk to a mere 100.

Of course in 1889 the old manorial system was just coming to its end, when the tenants acquired the freehold and the freedom to farm the land just as they pleased.

Even today the land is still very fertile, but it would be nice to put the clock back and see the individual strips planted as they once were with red clover, wheat, rye, peas, beans, potatoes, turnips and vetches – all in ¼ acre strips.

Or see all the village turn out to help at harvest time when there was a bumper crop of barley and they wanted to gather it in before the autumn rains started to fall!

47

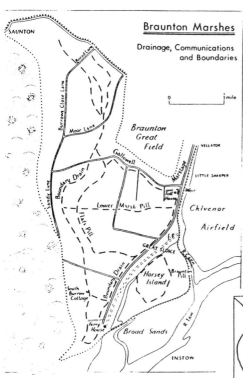

Braunton Marshes

Drainage, Communications
and Boundaries

— *before it was reclaimed*

Map of the Marsh

— *after it was reclaimed*

SAUNTON

Broad Lane

Burrows Close Lane

Moor Lane

Braunton Great Field

Gallowell

VELLATOR

Sandy Lane

Boundary Drain

LITTLE SHARPER

Toll House

Weir

Chivenor Airfield

Flats Pill

Lower Marsh Pill

Nortleigh

GREAT SLUICE

R.E.E.

R.E.E.

Boundary Drain

Horsey Island

Braunton Pill

South Burrow Cottage

Ferry House

Broad Sands

R. Taw

INSTOW

E

E

25

Saunton Road

Brau

E

S

Swanpool

Braunton Great Field

Coen

25

25

Sir Arthur's Pill

Braunton

Velator Marsh

Wrafton Marsh

Sharper Marsh

Inner Marsh Pill

Marsh

Wrafton

Flats Pill

Marsh

Bow Weir

South Burrows Marsh

Broad Sands

Horsey Island

Braunton Pill

Braunton

Burrows

River Taw

0.5 km

Bench Hill

Mouth of the Coen

MLW

25

MLW

Yelland Marsh

N

..... Salt Marsh Boundary   — · — · Parish Boundary

— — — Brackish Marsh Boundary   MLW   Mean Low Water

The Marshes

At the southern edge of the Great Field, separated by the Saxon's blackthorn hedge, lies the lush pastureland of Braunton Marsh. Here, at first glance, you are tempted into believing that this peaceful area has always been as it looks today, with its contented, plump cattle, wild flowers, and the families of ducks that paddle around in the drainage channels.

It is true that nature did play her part in shaping this attractive marshland, but the ingenuity of man tamed and altered her original work, making it into what you see today.

Cattle have been grazed here for centuries, but until the marsh was reclaimed in 1811, the quality of its pastures was poor, and the stock were in constant danger of being drowned by the incoming tides, for it was a vast, wild, tidal, salt-marsh.

Across it stretched an intricate net-work of tidal creeks, allowing salt water to penetrate into the very heart of the marsh, even if the tide was merely a slow 'neap'. And, with fortnightly, swifter, higher ones, the whole marsh became just one waterlogged lake.

Then the cattle would be herded onto higher ground, usually by young boys, who, when doing so, often missed their footing on the edge of one of the deep creeks, and so they, along with the cattle were drowned.

Sometimes, cattle wandered off the marsh of their own accord, either in search of lusher pastures, or driven by an incoming tide. Such trespass often caused arguments, bad feeling, and letters of complaint.

One such letter was written in 1793 by Mr P R Webber, who was the squire of Buckland at the time, to John Cleveland, Lord of the Manor of Saunton, at the way cattle invaded his fields on the east side of the marsh, at Burrows Close Lane. In it he said "I can no longer suffer the daily and hourly trespass I receive from your tenant . . . by which means the Produce of my Estate is continually devoured by all the Marsh Stock. My servants drive out of it several times a day near one hundred head of cattle of all sorts".

That this marsh was greatly overstocked during the eighteenth century there can be little doubt when you look at such figures as six (of the Courtney tenants) grazed 16 horses, 32 cattle and 320 sheep, and there were more than thirty such tenants using the marsh in this manor alone (Braunton Abbots). The other manors that owned land on the marsh were Braunton: Gorges (the Rolles), Gorges/Arundell (Bassetts), and

The Great Sluice on the seaward side

on the landward side

Saunton (Cleveland) together with the people who had grazing rights attached to their farms, making the ownership of the Marsh a complicated mosaic that echoed the Great Field. In addition, the upper west portion was common land that everyone was entitled to use.

In 1808, a man called Vancouver recommended that this salt marsh would benefit from being reclaimed. And when he pointed out that such a measure would greatly increase the value of the land, 'reclaimation mania' broke out, and various meetings were held by the interested parties. Some came up with wild schemes for dealing with even more than the 1200 acres that Vancouver thought was ready for reclaiming. But others were not so enthusiastic.

Before them were the plans that had been drawn up by an engineer called James Green, which put forward two alternative schemes. One was for the 1200 acres that Vancouver suggested, while the other, a more modest affair, proposed a sea bank which started at Broadsands, and continued for a three mile stretch ending at Velator.

As with any scheme which envelopes several interested parties, decisions were only finally agreed upon after a great deal of wrangling and arguments had taken place. Also, before work could start, an Act of Parliament was necessary, but eventually, after three years, the Act was passed, and work on the amended, more modest scheme, could begin.

It involved building a massive barrier – The Great Sea Bank – between Broad Sands, close to today's White House, or to give it its 'updated title' – Crow Beach House, and Marstage Farm, that would make 949 acres free from the ravages of the sea.

As there was not enough local labour, men were drafted in from Cornwall, Ireland and Holland, to complete the task, which cost £20,000, and took four years. The bank was built a hundred feet thick in places, to withstand the harsh conditions it would have when extra high tides were backed by fearsome gale force winds. It was divided into five sections by walls in which there were gates across the Toll Road, and stiles on its summit, for there was a footpath along its top.

To maintain their newly acquired drainage, and cope with the constant flow of fresh water that ran down from Saunton and Lobb, a net-work of artificial delphs were dug out, whose water levels were maintained by a series of sluice gates, the most impressive being the Great Sluice on the seaward side. All the existing tidal creeks were retained, like Sir Arthur's Pill, only now the water flowed one way, towards the sea.

Altogether twelve miles of these drainage channels were created, for which the Dutch labour proved to be very useful, as they were very similar to those that existed in Holland.

Marsh Commissioners and Inspectors were appointed to look after the management of the area, and three houses were built for them. One was the White House, and another was at South Barrow. The third was the Toll House where the toll-keeper lived, whose job it was to collect 2d, quite a large sum in those days, from every horse-drawn cart that passed on the way to Broadsands.

During the busy tourist season, the toll keepers can be seen busily opening and shutting the toll gate for modern forms of transport that would have astonished the people who built their home, for this area is very popular not only with the holiday makers, but also with the local people.

The newly reclaimed marshland was divided into 130 allotments by fences, walls, and gates, with bridges across the drainage channels. And the Marsh and Toll Roads were made.

Once all the work was finished, people viewed its future with mixed feelings. During the time when it was being reclaimed all the grazing stock had been removed. The rents of the tenants were reduced "for being deprived of the advantages of the marsh". But this did not compensate them completely, for anyone owning alternative grazing was able to cash in, which they did, and charge 2/6 (15p) a week per beast.

And this was not the only shock in store for the tenants. To pay for the costs of the work, and to extinguish the common rights, all the manorial tenants were obliged to buy their plots of land, varying in size according to extent of their original holding. But after 99 years everything reverted back to the landlord. Other plots were sold, under the same terms, to anyone who applied for them.

Some of these plots were very small, which resulted in gross overstocking, with the subsequent grazing becoming so poor that marsh farmers complained that there seemed nothing they could do to make the grazing palatable for their stock.

Some farmers turned to crops instead. From 1819 to 1822, records show that wheat, barley and "pease" that had been grown on the marsh were sold by auction at the Black Horse. But obviously it was not very successful, for by 1824 these same owners were sowing clovers, "cock grass", and "everseed" (the local term for rye-grass) in readiness for grazing stock once more.

To maintain the safety of the marsh, the sea wall came under strict regulations. Pigs, being a rooting animal, were specially mentioned, for they would seriously damage its structure. Owners who allowed such beasts to wander near, or on the bank, were fined 10/- per animal. Rats,

The Great Sea bank alongside the Toll Road

Toll Gate

moles and other undermining vermin were tightly controlled, and in 1829, a Mr James Day was fined 4/6 "as a mitagated punishment for riding on the Bank".

But later, when the grass took root on the bank creating what is known as a 'closed sward' a limited number of sheep were allowed to graze it, and became regarded as being the most efficient means of maintaining it.

By 1853 Mr William Williams had become the owner of the Heanton Estate. Unlike the previous owners, the Bassetts, he was very keen to have the Wrafton Marshes reclaimed, for although as lords of the manor of Gorges and Arundell, they had co-operated with the enclosure of the Braunton Marsh, they were the main objectors to the more extensive venture that Vancouver had put forward, which involved the Heanton Estate.

But now Mr Williams went even further, for he proposed that alterations should be made to the River Caen, which at that time flowed out to the sea, quite separate from the Pill, near the White House side of Horsey Island, after wending its way across Sharper and Wrafton Marsh.

What he suggested was that the River Caen be straightened, to stop it from meandering round Sharper Marsh, and that the Wrafton Knowle water should be made to join it at Velator Bridge. This river should then be made to enter the Taw through the Pill with its previous estuary being blocked by a Sea Bank. This second Sea Bank would cut into the existing one near the White House, when it would curve around Horsey Island, ending around the corner at Pills Mouth, where it would again link with the end of the existing Great Sea Bank. At this time a new Marsh had developed in the upper regions of Horsey Island, making it ripe for such a venture. The Wrafton Marsh would be reclaimed by a similar bank which would follow the curve of the land along the banks of the Taw and up the Pill.

And this is what they did. The new Sea Banks that were on the seaward side were made with a slope of 1 in 5 in the form of a pebble ridge, to minimise the battering they would receive from the waves. The other banks were made of puddled clay, into which pitch-paving was driven, along with stones that had been quarried from Braunton Down, and estuary boulders. When this second massive sea defence was completed, the costs of the two systems together amounted to a staggering £60,000 – what would this be today?

In June, 1857 the final gap which would prevent the sea from entering the old mouth of the Caen, was closed. It took 320 men, with 140 carts, working non-stop, in between two tides.

The Marsh Keeper's House

Workers who repaired the Great Sea Bank

Today if you stand on this Sea Bank near the White House and walk along looking down at the stonework which filled this final gap, you cannot help but marvel at their ingenuity, knowing that once a broad river flowed through the spot on which you are standing. Looking back toward Horsey Island, you can still see a difference in the vegetation indicating the path where the Caen once flowed.

To mark the occasion a day's general holiday was declared. After all, they had tamed a river, not to mention winning the age-old battle with the sea.

Unfortunately their triumph did not last for ever, for in 1910, on Friday, 23rd December, disaster struck. It had been blowing a gale throughout the day, but early in the afternoon it increased to almost a hurricane. It was an extra high tide, which, when it reached its peak (or top) at 5.24 pm, was already causing a tremendous amount of damage all around the coastal regions of North Devon. The newspaper reports at the time speak of waves at places like Ilfracombe pounding the harbour with awesome force, before flying up into undreamt of heights.

At about 6 pm there was a huge tidal wave. Suddenly the great sea banks gave way in three places, and a huge gap developed in the one that protected Horsey Island, allowing the tide to surge on through towards the other Great Sea Bank, which also gave way. The Heanton Sea Bank also was breached, and the village of Chivenor became flooded, with some houses being awash in nearly twelve feet of water.

With few exceptions, every animal perished that had been grazing on the reclaimed marshland in that dark evening of disaster. Next morning, the farmers looked at the scene of devastation, for lying on their once fertile pasture land, amongst the sand, seaweed and gravel deposited by the sea, lay hundreds of dead sheep, partridges and rabbits.

Local opinion blamed the constant burrowing of the rabbits in the Great Sea Banks for their failure to withstand the storm, but from the newspaper reports of the damage that occurred at Ilfracombe, Combe Martin, Clovelly, Lynmouth and Lee, it seems that it was the terrible power of the hurricane blown tide, and the final huge wave that made such a mockery of the sea defences.

Most of the linhays were wrecked, with one exception, in which three surviving sheep were found, huddled together. It brought financial ruin to many, and has been blamed for being responsible for the sharp decline in the fortunes of Sir Frederick Williams.

In all this disaster there was just one amusing feature. A farm labourer was surprised to find surviving rabbits crouching in the tree tops. They must have scrambled up there for safety, but were too afraid to jump down.

Mud flats at Pill's End

Farmers after the flood

It was nearly a year before the Great Sea Banks were repaired, and great holes, some twenty feet deep, developed at Pill's Mouth, making it a death trap for shipping. One vessel, a barge called the "Shamrock", sunk in one of them. Another, larger vessel, called the "TMP" became drawn into a gap in the Great Sea Bank, and landed up on the marsh, where she continued to float because the water was so deep. When the tide went out, they managed to navigate her out with it.

It took 100,000 tons of material to breach the gap, at a total cost of £10,000.

Today, the Great Sea Banks are covered with grass, and the marshland is home to a great number of animals, birds and wild flowers. There are dropwort, hogweed, meadow sweet, black mustard and charlock growing in the drainage channels, and dragon-flies can be seen hovering above the water. Flag iris provides a wonderful splotch of yellow as it nestles amongst the clumps of sharp sea rushes. Ducks and swans have made their homes here, where salt-marsh plants like sea milkwort and sea arrow grass still thrive, despite being deprived of salt water since 1910. Wild flowers, such as common sorrel and buttercup, ripple in a riot of reds and yellows as a skylark adds its voice to the summer sounds. This pastureland has become a sanctuary for wildfowl, lapwings, common snipes and golden plover, and, if you are there at dusk, you may catch a glimpse of a barn owl as he searches for voles or field mice.

In the summer, you will see today's plump-bellied cattle munching the much improved pasture land, which is now considered to be the best beef-fattening land in the West of England, with some fine examples of the old traditional "Devon Reds".

Dotted across the marshes are barns and linhays that vary in shape and size. Next to the Marsh Road is a splendid example of a circular linhay that is of great historic interest, for this type is unique to Devon. The roof has now been renovated after it collapsed during a gale in 1981.

Other buildings are rectangular, and are made of coarse rubble with slated roofs. Once they had walled enclosures against flooding into which cattle would be driven, and the entrances sealed up with clay and stones.

This flat, spacious pastureland stretches, as far as the eye can see to the distant sand dunes; the largest area of its kind in Great Britain. Hopefully, the Sea Banks will never again be breached, for Braunton Marshes and Horsey Island are now included in the Taw and Torridge site of Special Scientific Interest. It is undoubtedly a place of great charm and character in which nature and man has conspired to create something that is both functional and pleasant to look at.

Circular linhay near Marsh Road

"Maud", "Bessie Gould" and the "Enid" moored at Rolle Quay

The "Hilda" last of the old sailing barges

Velator and its Shipping Trade

There was an old saying amongst the Braunton sailors that: "The Lord sends the grub – but the Devil supplies the cook". This just about sums up their down to earth attitude to life, for they were a tough breed, those Braunton sailors. They had to be, to cope with the dangers, and hardships of Braunton's seafaring trade.

From time immemorial Braunton men have been sailors, but until the course of the Caen was altered, the size of their vessels had always been limited. Now that the river Caen flowed out into the Taw via Pills Mouth, they could use craft of up to 130 tons. Also the handling of their cargoes would be more efficient, with the help of the smart new quay that had been built at Velator.

And so dawned the era when the upsurge of Braunton's seagoing trading made one historian describe it as "A village with one leg in its farmlands and the other in the sea". But there was one obstacle that they never would be able to control and that was the weather, for often contrary winds would keep a vessel port bound, either at Braunton, or away across the Bristol Channel in one of the Welsh ports. And with the Taw and Torridge estuary, there was always the Barnstaple/Bideford Bar to contend with (no one can ever seem to agree about this particular name). This is a huge sand bank that has been formed by the constant movements of the two rivers and the sea. Navigation of this bar is crucial, and even today you will still see, if you look down from the main road at Saunton, vessels waiting for the tide to give them enough 'draught' (water beneath them) to clear this natural obstacle.

In the old days they had to do this without the aid of motors, with only wind-power, and to miss this 'spring', as it was called, often meant great financial hardship for the sailors' families. Often, sailors' wives would use the excuse that "Maister's lost his spring," so that they could have credit in the village shops.

In fact, very often the families of the seamen suffered almost as much as their menfolk, especially when a safe return was overdue. This is probably the reason that superstitions were not laughed at in a profession that was fraught with so many dangers. Women were considered very unlucky aboard ship, and so were kept firmly at home. They rarely renamed a ship, for it was considered to bring about a disaster, and even the vessels themselves were looked upon as being a safe, lucky ship, or a troublesome-always-needing-constant-attention-liability.

Most of Braunton's shipping was coastal, so familiar landmarks were used as navigational aids, especially with the estuaries, where the deep channels would have to be followed. These can be clearly seen at

"Bessie Gould" moored at Velator

The Clarke family

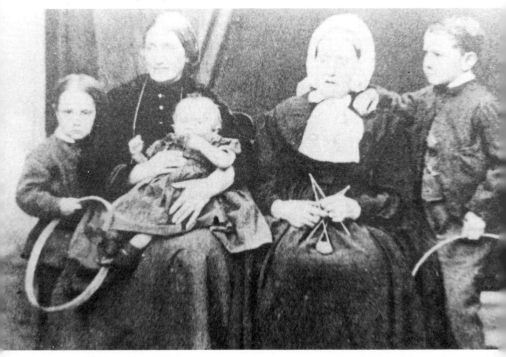

low tides, running through the sand banks, but ships do not sail at low tide, so their whereabouts had to be known by other means.

One such landmark was St. Michael's Chapel, which contrary to popular belief, is not the ruined version of St Brannock's attempt to build a church. There was in fact a seamen's chapel there long before the great upsurge in Braunton's seagoing trade. Sailors' wives would go there to pray for the safe return of their menfolk, and a light was kept burning there as a navigational aid for homeward bound seamen.

One vantage point that the wives used as a lookout was the site of the old Beacon, on West Hill. There the women would gather, and when they spotted the ships approaching the bar, they would sucrry along South Street to Velator to meet their husbands. Not because they desired to give them a homecoming kiss, but because they wanted to relieve them of most of their wages before they could spend the lot in the "Mariners' Arms"!

During the heyday of Braunton's seagoing trade many names have become legendary, and in St Brannock's Church they have been preserved, for most of them are inlaid into walls, written on wooden blocks. Other authors have named these men, so this book will not attempt the task, and will concentrate on the sort of life that these tough seafaring men led.

Once the shipping trade was underway, most of the interested parties tended to make their homes in South Street, where their favourite 'watering hole' was the Mariner's Arms. It became a headquarters to these men, who used it to sign on crews or exchange seafaring yarns. It would be wonderful to travel back in time so that you could hear some of the tall stories that were told over a pint of ale!

That the seagoing trade was brisk can be seen by the number of vessels that sailed from Velator between 1860 and the end of the Second World War. During those years over 100 vessels, some up to 60 tons, carried a diversity of cargoes to and from this busy 'port', going to such far flung places as Ireland and even America. There were also 10 sand barges that dredged their cagoes from the sea-bed for the building industry, and this continues to this day. Watching one of these sand barges coming up the river fully loaded, you will not be the first person to wonder how on earth the vessel manages to float, sitting so low in the water.

Velator's waterside area became alive with sailors going to, or coming from their ships. The road often suffered major traffic jams as the air rang with the clatter of the horses' hooves that pulled the cartloads of cargoes to and from the berthed vessels.

These ships were mostly manned by Braunton men, and there was never any shortage of willing volunteers, for there were always more men than vessels. In fact, it was not that easy to 'just go to sea', for the majority of these ships were crewed as family affairs. The boys were taught their seamanship from a very early age, and, as the entire crew sometimes only numbered three, everyone was expected to take turns at the wheel, or help to load, or unload the cargoes. It was only in the larger vessels that you found a definite division of labour.

But even on these vessels, the lads joined them at around 12½ to 13, and were expected to knuckle under and be prepared to work long hours. They were taught to steer the ship through all types of weather, be able to tie any sort of knot, handle the sails, or scrub down the decks. And, with the smaller ships, they quickly became initiated into the mysteries of cooking.

By the time they reached fifteen, aboard the large, or the small ships, they were first class sailors, and many left the area to continue their apprenticeships elsewhere, for their years under sail with the Braunton sailors were such an excellent reference, that they were able to obtain a job in any class of ship. Sometimes, they went on to become naval officers, or took on the responsible, and skilful job of pilot in another port.

The overall conditions aboard a Braunton vessel depended very much on the temperament of the skipper (known locally as the 'mate' – but sometimes 'skipper'). A good mate, and you would have a happy ship, but a bad one, and the crew's resentment would undermine efficiency, and therefore the safety of the vessel.

The hours were often very long, for there was always so much to do. And even when resting, the shout, "All hands on deck", meant the loss of a night's sleep. A sailor's rota was divided into sea 'watches'. This would be four hours on, and four hours off. In harbour, it was 6 to 6.

Often, sailors would confess that during a long, slogging passage in the winter, when a howling gale was lashing torrential rain into their faces, and they were fighting to keep the ship on an even keel, they would vow to become a 'land-lubber'. But, after twelve hours on dry land, with a full belly, and a pint of foaming ale at their lips, they would forget all about these hardships, as they yarned away in the "Mariner's Arms". Then, they only remembered the compensations, as they romanced about the thrills they remembered during the summer, when, with a favourable, strong breeze, they had sailed past all the other slower ships, with their vessel skimming through the surf, sails billowing and flapping, and its timbers creaking, as though she was alive and was enjoying the thrills as much as the sailors. And, their reminiscences did not end there, for as a sailor bent his head, and his bristly whiskers skimmed off the top of his pint, he would speak of the character, beauty, wisdom and strength that you found in a good ship, manned by a willing, competent crew.

It must have been a lively place the "Mariner's Arms", with all those tough men warming themselves by its huge log fire. Of course, in such a gathering you would find an atmosphere of rivalry, for everyone was proud of their own seamanship, and their undying love for their ships.

They would often brag who could set up the sails the best, and in the shortest time. But there was also valuable gossip that added to the store of local knowledge. You would probably have heard things like "Did you know, that such and such gut (channel of deep water) had altered this way, or that, in last night's storm?" Or, "That such and such sand bank is now bigger – or smaller?"

But the competition for cargoes was taken seriously, for the men's pay depended on their quality. But, in a tight spot, if anyone was in trouble, all differences were quickly forgotten, and it was "All hands on deck", to help in any way that was possible.

Food aboard these ships was viewed as being of the upmost importance. They ate well, even if there was very little variety. A typical day's menu would be:

Breakfast – Dried cod (toe rag) or roller oats (barque) followed by coffee

Dinner – boiled brisket of beef, with potatoes, cabbage or swede or scouse – a 'species' of stew.

Not forgetting everybody's favourite – Figgy Duff (A seagoing version of spotted dick or plum pudding).

With, if no one had annoyed the dreaded cook, a cake for tea, or a biscuit (hard-tack) and bread, with butter and jam. And a cup of tea.

Between 1910, and the 1930s, forty ships regularly traded with the Bristol Channel ports. About twelve of these vessels were known as "Traders", and were between 60 to 80 tons and were ketch rigged. They carried gravel from Braunton to Swansea, Cardiff, Barry, Newport, Bristol, Gloucester, Porline, Llanelly, Minehead and Ilfracombe.

Sometimes, they returned to Barnstaple, rather than Velator, and carried mostly coal for household use, or for the Gas and Electric Companies. But also, salt, manure or flour, and miller's produce would be shipped into Barnstaple or Braunton.

The runs of these ships tended to follow a set pattern throughout the year, for they used the same merchants. Because Braunton was never classed as a port, they all had to be registered at Barnstaple.

There were also the larger vessels, 90 to 120 tons, that made the round trip, loaded with gravel from Braunton up the Bristol Channel to one of the Welsh ports, returning home with roadstone from Porthgain. These larger ships were called 'coasters' and were nearly all schooners.

In the summer months some of the smaller ships would go further than the Bristol Channel, looking for potential cargoes if their usual 'home trade' became slack, or to places that were only accessible during the better weather.

Life for these Braunton sailors was hard, for there was no such thing as regular hours; it all depended on the dictates of the tide. Arriving in port on the high water, the sails would have to be stowed away, and then it would be 'all hands on deck', to make ready for discharging the cargoes over the side as soon as the tide was far enough out.

Carts would clatter alongside the vessel, and then the off loading would continue without a break until the ship's hold was empty. By this time, the tide would have turned again, and the vessel would have to be made ready to move off once more.

The cargoes they carried varied, but were made up mostly of clay, coal, pitch, road metal, crushed granite, gravel, salt, malt, oats, cement, manure, phosphate, scrap iron, railway sleeper, potatoes, pit props, and timber.

One feature that no one can fail to notice, dotted all along the North Devon coastline, and up and down the river banks, are the derelict lime kilns. In the days when the farmers relied on lime to sweeten the soil, these kilns were in constant use just prior to the yearly liming of the soil.

The raw limestone came from Caldy Island in South Wales, and when the Braunton sailors were spotted approaching the bar from the top of West Hill, the carts would clatter down to Velator to wait for them to berth. Competition for this limestone was fierce, for there was not always enough to go around.

Some seamen also helped on the farms, and this combination gave rise to the term, "The Braunton teddy-diggers". Others doubled up as watermen–labourers, and became known as "hobblers'. But whatever task they undertook, there was nothing in the way of creature comforts that seamen enjoy today.

Accommodation in most of these vessels was very poor, and often cramped. With the smaller ships, the cooking was done in the forecastle (foc'sle) which doubled up as living space, crew's sleeping quarters, boatswain's (bo'sun's) store, chain locker, and if the need ever arose – as a

Modern Velator   *What would the old sea-salts say?*

The 'basin' at Velator

prison. When they fitted engines to these vessels, living space became even more cramped, because they made the master's cabin into the engine room, so he then also moved into the forecastle.

Even the dangers of the Second World War did not deter the Braunton seamen. Many joined the Royal Navy, where their homespun expertise took them quickly through the ranks. Others joined the Merchant Navy and risked their lives on the convoys which the German Fleet attacked so visciously. The ones that stayed at home continued to sail the Bristol Channel, carrying scrap metal from bomb torn Bristol across to Wales, and their vigilant coal runs kept more than one home fire burning.

But of all the seafaring tales of Braunton, the most romantic is its association with the *Result*. In her heyday, she was considered to be the finest sailing vessel in the coasting trade. Originally, she was rigged as a topsail schooner with doubled topsails on the fore.

In 1909 she was bought by J. Clarke, and was first sailed up the Pill by Sid Incledon. She was the largest vessel (122 tons) to ever come up this river, so it is not too difficult to imagine that most of the villagers probably turned out to see her!

During the 1914–18 War she was one of a number of merchant vessels that were taken over by the Admiralty to be fitted out as 'Q' ships, to try to combat the German Submarine menace. The *Result* was commissioned at Lowestoft in January 1917 as HMS *Dag* Q.23, and her commanding officer was Lt PJ Mack RN, with Lt G Mulhauser, and a crew of 24. By this time she already had an engine, but now they fitted her with two 12-pounder guns, and two 12 inch torpedo tubes.

But outwardly, the *Result* still appeared to be an ordinary merchant vessel, engaged in innocent trading, rather than a commissioned vessel that was manned by Royal Naval personnel. The idea was that she would lure the submarines close enough to be in range of her guns, then she would hoist the White Ensign, and open fire.

She fought in two major actions. The first was in February 1917, off the Outer Silver Pit at the tail of the Dogger Bank. There she found a German U.45 submarine. In the resulting exchange, the *Result* claimed to have sunk the German ship, but found out later that she had managed to limp back home, but the Captain, and three of her crew were dead.

Her second battle was at the North Hinder Lightship. This time, it was a bigger submarine – with bigger guns. But this did not deter the *Result*, she still went into the attack. If pluck could win victories she would have sunk this German submarine, but as it turned out, she had taken on more than she could cope with. The German ship had nearly

*"The Result" under full sail
as "Flash" in "Outcasts of the Islands"*

The "Result" being lifted into retirement

finished her off, when two RN destroyers, returning from a sweep in the North Sea, sailed to her rescue.

Two heavy plates were needed to repair the damage done by the shellfire, but then she was back at sea again looking for more submarines. By the summer of 1917, HMS Q.23 was finally paid off, and could return to the quieter life of a coasting schooner, proudly bearing her 'war wounds', two large steel plates, that could be clearly seen about her water-line.

She was now owned by the Welch family and became a familiar sight as she sailed majestically up the Pill, loaded with cargo and crewed by Braunton men.

Today this proud ship has returned to Ireland where she was built, by Paul Rogers of Carrickfergus, and is on permanent display at a Folk Museum in Ulster, her sailing days over, but still playing a role as a reminder of the romantic days of the sailing ships.

Today Velator is a peaceful place. No longer is it Braunton's busy waterside area. Pleasure boats, owned by weekend sailors, wearing yellow wellies, are moored up along the banks that were once used by the schooners and ketches.

There is a car park there now, used by the tourists and the locals who walk along the same bank which once the Braunton seaman walked. And the council has landscaped and grassed over an area where you can sit down and enjoy the view. Beneath this grass are buried several wrecks, but people who remember the role they played in Braunton's life will never forget them – for we are an island people and the bravery of our young men, and their skilful seamanship, has saved us from an aggressor on more than one occasion.

"Sailor's Day"

Braunton sailors had their own way of dealing with unwanted interference. It was on a bleak November's Sunday in 1931. The ketch *Ann* loaded up with coal came up the Pill. She was owned by Thommy Slee and was captained by Robert Parkhouse. As she approached Velator Quay to unload her cargo, her crew were surprised to find that the area was fenced off, and so it was impossible to discharge her coal. Also, a hut had appeared in the area.

Word was sent to Thommy Slee, who in the true Braunton tradition, was up in arms about this contravention to the seamen's right, for by an ancient charter that was granted to them for the role that Braunton's sailors had played in the Spanish War, they would always have free moorings, and the right to unload without hindrance at Velator.

With this ancient right firmly fixed in his mind, Thomas Slee cut the padlock and tore down the fence that had been erected by a Mr William Isaac, who intended to extract levies from the Braunton seamen for the privilege of using the quayside. And just for good measure, Thommy Slee demolished the smart new hut.

By this time, 500 villagers had arrived to watch the spectacle, along with the village policeman. After their demolition job, Thommy Slee and his mates proceeded to off load the ship, and then went home, or into

71

the "Mariners Arms" to enjoy a pint, and laugh about the whole affair.

But it did not seem so funny when they each received a summons for their stand against the infringement of their ancient rights. Thomas Slee and his helpers: Robert Parkhouse, "Shada" Bill Mullen, George Coates, Stan Rogers and Bill Mitchell were taken to court on August 23rd. They were all found guilty of malicious damage to property, and were fined a grand total of £7. So the sailors appealed against the sentence in the High Court – and their case was upheld. Today a notice appears at the quayside which states:

> "This quay is the property of Braunton Council. Public rights of mooring on the quay are for the purpose of loading and unloading and emergency repairs only. There is no right to moor permanently or for any other purpose. Vessels are requested to move to other moorings as soon as possible after carrying out these functions in order not to interfere with the rights of others. Vessels must not moor on the slipway or obstruct the navigation channel."

From then on, the day when Thommy Slee and his fellow vandals cocked a snook at the law, has always been known in Braunton's seafaring lore, as "Sailor's Day".

In the churchyard of St Brannock's church near the path from the north gate can be found the grave of a William Gray. He was surgeon of HMS *Weazel* a Brig-of-War that was wrecked in a north-westerly gale on the rocks of Baggy in 1799.

A mystery surrounds the wrecking of this vessel because she had spent some time at Appledore where her crews became very friendly with the locals, especially the ladies. This sociability led the Captain ,the Hon Henry Grey, to throw a party on the night before the Brig sailed. For reasons that can only be speculative the *Weazel* abruptly sailed from Appledore at first light the following morning, Sunday 10th February, leaving one crew-man behind. On board, presumably from the party, was a woman who tradition claims was called Nancy Golding.

Her abrupt departure is strange because ships rarely sailed on a Sunday but one explanation that has been suggested by Mr Norman Fulford is that she sailed to avoid trouble because she was engaged in press-ganging. Mr Fulford recalls a relative of his mother's, a sea captain, disappeared from the "Prince of Wales" pub having been press-ganged. And this could have been the reason for the party, so that local men could be plied with liquor to such extent that they would have woken up sober and at sea.

Another theory is that the *Weazel* was trying to apprehend one of the smuggling gangs who operated in the area, and this was the reason she cast off so abruptly from Appledore, because she learnt of a homecoming smuggling vessel laden with contraband.

Villagers all along the coastal region of North Devon saw the *Weazel* when they were going to church. By the time the services were over the *Weazel* was in trouble, and was firing distress flares as the north westerly gale forced her towards the jagged rocks of Baggy headland. The sound of these distress flares continued into the evening until 1am, when they abruptly fell silent. Next morning all that remained of the *Weazel* was floating wreckage scattered in the waves on the Croyde side of Baggy.

Of her crew which numbered 106 only a handful were ever found, washed ashore at Croyde, and were buried at Georgeham. By the time these bodies were appearing a request arrived from the Admiralty to save the ship's stores and fittings. This salvage operation was organised by a Richard Bugg who in accordance with Admiralty instructions held a public auction which made £80.

Today nothing remains of the Hospital Ship which was moored off Broad Sands at Crow between 1893 and 1927. In those days such ships were used as isolation units for homecoming seamen who had contracted infectious diseases in foreign ports so were often found in busy seafaring estuaries such as the Taw and Torridge.

Braunton's local population became alarmed after a vessel called the "Fortunato Repetto" arrived at Appledore flying the yellow "fever" flag, for she had returned from the infected East Indian port of Bahia.

Three years later the Port Health Sanitary Authority authorised the purchase of a ship that would be suitable for use as a Hospital Ship. The French vessel *Nymphen* was selected at a cost of £275. For her voyage from France to Appledore she was insured for £400! At Appledore her surplus stores were auctioned and she was re-fitted as an Infectious Diseases Hospital. 'Air-conditioning' was provided by wind-vanes mounted on the deckhouse which could be revolved by hand wheels which fed fresh air into a trunk which extended right down to the bilge deck. She had a male and female ward, an isolation ward, and two convalescent wards. Below these wards were the nurses' bathroom and toilet, the kitchen and the scullery. Apart from the usual furnishing of beds and commodes she had three Bodley ranges fitted.

When she was settled into her berth at Broad Sands she was ballasted with gravel and her rigging was removed and they painted on her "Barnstaple Port Sanitary Hospital".

Once the ship was ready arrangements were made for someone to look after her, and their duties were specified.

1   To look after the Ship and her mooring, and report from time to time as to anything necessary to be done.
2   To do any repairs such as hardening deck seams, painting, or any small repairs.
3   To keep the Wards clean and tidy and the linen aired.
4   To keep an account of the Water supply and give timely notice of its growing short.
5   Attend to the Sanitary arrangements and generally carry out the suggestions of the Medical Officer of Health in that direction.
6   To keep all the taps & closets clean
7   When Nurses and patients are on Board to attend to the Stove, carry coals, clean Nurses' Boots, and in every way assist the Nurses.
8   The Caretaker's Wife to keep the Linen and crockery clean and in order , also to cook for the patients and Nurses when required and if capable to nurse in a simple case.

Charles Perterick was given this task helped by his wife Hester, and later in the 1920's, to a Mr Burgess an ex-naval man and his wife.

With all these preparations the only patient who was ever nursed there was a Able Seaman Basset, who in 1903 was taken off the vessel *Bessie Gould* because he was suffering from smallpox. According to my mother when she was child, another seaman had smallpox and died of it in South Street which caused a lot of comment in the village because he was never admitted to the Hospital Ship.

When the Great Sea Wall gave way in the storm of 1910 the *Nymphen* dragged her anchors and had to be hauled inshore once more with hawsers.

By 1924 the *Nymphen* was joined by another Hospital Ship called *Charlotte* which seems amazing considering the shortage of patients. Two years later the Authority ordered a survey on both ships and they were sold to Hinks of Appledore in June 1927 for £32!

Salvaging a cannon from a wreck

The lads of Braunton have always been noted for their high spirits, and often this zest for life has led them into trouble. This happened on Good Friday in 1918 when they became involved in a spot of wrecking. Word reached the village that a schooner called the *Volent* was ashore on Saunton beach after her steering gear had failed at Hartland Point.

It was whispered there was no one on board her as her crew had been rescued by the Appledore lifeboat. The boys agreed that they would be doing the ship's owner a favour if all the valuables could be removed before the tide came in. After all, it was a time honoured custom to salvage what the sea brought in. And old habits die hard. Even the men were going to have a look, so it must be all right.

Before long, the stores and items like the lifebelts and the ship's foghorn were all whisked away back to the village. One boy marched up Caen Street blowing the foghorn as he went along. This alerted Sergeant Robinson to what was happening, so he immediately shouted for the boys to accompany him to the station, but he was ignored. Then he gave chase, and the boys scattered in all directions; not that it mattered, for he knew who the culprits were.

The court case was heard in Barnstaple. All the men and boys who were involved faced a steely faced magistrate who was not at all amused. Some of the property had been returned to the owners, but the remainder was never recovered. Of the men, most were acquitted, but others later went to Exeter and the Devon Quarter Sessions. And the boys? They were allowed to go free, for the magistrate considered that their elders had set them a bad example. But before they were allowed to walk out of the court-room he could not resist saying, "I shall remember each one of you, and if I ever see your faces in this court-room again, your feet will not touch the ground".

Huge whale washed ashore at Saunton

Being a closely knit community, news always travelled very swiftly if anything interesting was washed ashore in the estuary or the nearby beaches, so when a huge, dead whale was discovered, opposite the lifeboat house at Saunton on 27th December, in 1911, people were only too willing to go and inspect it. No one knew if the whale had been alive when it first became beached, but it was clearly dead by the time Mr Baglow discovered it. Being winter-time, the weather was bitterly cold, but this did not deter the villagers, who flocked to have a look at the now foul smelling fifty foot carcase with its enormous tail.

Once the initial excitement was over, the rotting whale became something of an embarrassment, for it was classed as a "Royal Fish", that was known as "Droits of the Admiralty", so no one was allowed to touch it.

Eventually, the evil smell forced the issue, and common sense made the Custom's authorities deal with it. For many years the skull of this huge fish was on show, on the Croyde side of Baggy Point, reminding us what huge creatures must often swim in the Bristol Channel unseen, unless some disaster befalls them.

The old lighthouse – 1907

The Braunton Burrows

The Braunton Burrows are one of the largest areas of sand dunes in Great Britain, for they extend the three mile length of Saunton Beach, and for over a mile inland, where they meet the Marshes. They are internationally famous for their plant and animal life and have been fascinating scientists and naturalists since the 17th century.

Owned by the Christie Estate Trustees, two thirds have been made into a National Nature Reserve, while the southern end, near Broad Sands, has been leased to the Ministry of Defence since 1964. Here, notices warn you not to pass if you see a red flag flying, for squads of soliders with blackened faces will be playing war games.

The area is open to the public, who can gain access by two routes – one via the Toll Road, which brings you out at the White House, while the other is to turn off from the Saunton/Braunton Road (B3231), either by Burrows Close Lane, or Moor Lane, both of which link with Sandy Lane, which in turn leads to the American Road and a free car park.

Walking amongst these sand dunes, several interesting natural features can be seen – whole sea shells that have been dropped by the gulls as they carried them inland or, nearer to the shoreland, where they have been driven in by strong winds. Some dunes are lush with vegetation, while others are wind-blown sand hills anchored by graceful tough marram grass.

At Crow Point the land juts out to sea in the shape of a hook which is 25 feet high in places. This 'hook' is made of sand on which today marram grass grows. But it was not always like this, for it has been gradually formed since 1809. Recently it had to be repaired after it was breached by the sea, for this tongue of sand provides a valuable lee to the beach that stretches behind it and on towards Pills Mouth, from the main force of the tidal surge.

On the Braunton Burrows can be found over 400 different species of flowering plants, such as the horsebrake slack, wild pansy, and the sea holly. And, if anyone has the patience to sit quietly and watch, they may see rabbits, foxes, hedgehogs, moles, weazels, wild mink, shrews, voles and field mice.

As mentioned in an earlier chapter, the Braunton Burrows were so named after the Norman introduction of the rabbit, and prior to the spread of Myxomatosis in 1954, their vast numbers kept the vegetation at a much lower level than it is today. Since the dramatic drop in their population, the plants have steadily increased with each year.

Walking across the Braunton Burrows on a warm summer's day,

The Glos RAA boarding a train during World War 1

Crow Beach, and "Crow Beach House"

several different varieties of birds can be seen and heard, like pee-wits, magpies, kestrels, and even the occasional buzzard – hovering in search of his prey. And it is a butterflies' paradise.

There is a full time Warden, who, assisted by a number of volunteers, is only too willing to help visitors; arrange guided tours, or cater for educational parties.

The area has played its part in the nation's history, for in the First World War, the Glos. RAA were based at Sandy Lane, near West Saunton Farm. During the Second World War the American troops practised on the dunes in preparation for the Normandy landings, but this will be dealt with in more detail in another chapter.

Today, on Crow Beach, a modern, self-reliant navigational light is sited to aid shipping, and several well-equipped life- boats are stationed around the North Devon coast, to cope with stricken shipping. But, back in the eighteenth century the fate of sailors who sailed the Bideford/ Barnstaple Bay was a grim one, and countless wrecks came to grief for nobody could save them.

The first effort to do something was made in 1822, when a lighthouse was built on the sand dunes near Crow Point, and a lifeboat, the *Volunteer*, was stationed at Appledore in 1825. But still sailors perished when the lifeboat was unable to negotiate the Bar.

Then the North Devon Humane Society, patroned by Lord Rolle, was formed, and a second, 26ft long boat called the *Assistance*, was sent to Appledore. But still this did not solve the problem of going over the Bar in adverse conditions, so they decided to keep the *Assistance* at Airey Point on the Braunton side of the Barnstaple/Bideford Bay, on the seaward side of the Bar.

Two years later, a boat-house was built for the now firmly established Braunton Lifeboat Service. When the *Assistance* was needed, three guns were fired at Appledore, and then three rockets would be launched by the White House owner (who took care of the lifeboat station).

Once the Braunton people saw, or heard the gunfire and the rockets, men and horses would be gathered together, and the race to launch the lifeboat was on. Down the Saunton Road they galloped, towards the lifeboat station. In the meantime, the Appledore lifeboat crew rowed across the estuary, where, upon landing, they too raced towards Airey Point. By now the Braunton men would have arrived at the station, and would be using their horses to haul the lifeboat down over the sands and on, out, into the waves.

Braunton had six lifeboats during her life as a station. Some were donated by the RNLI, while others were given by wealthy, public

Preparing to launch the lifeboat

Braunton's Lifeboat Station

"Robert and Catherine" 1904

spirited people. This happened on August 25, 1881, when the *Robert & Catherine* was presented to the RNLI by a Miss Leicester of London. This boat replaced the *George & Catherine,* which had served the station since 1866. The new lifeboat was 34 feet in length and was 8 feet in breadth. She was transported from her builder's, Woolfe and Son, to Barnstaple by the South Western railway. Upon arrival at the station, she was taken aboard a carriage drawn by six horses, in a grand parade through the streets of Barnstaple, while the North Devon Yeomanry enthusiastically played "Hearts of Oak". They made it into a great day of celebration, with the new lifeboat being christened by Lady Susan Fortescue, before they carefully launched the *Robert & Catherine* into the Taw at a slipway on the South Walk.

This Miss Leicester was obviously a very public spirited lady, for she provided two further lifeboats (of the same name) in 1902 and 1912.

During the years that the lifebat was based at Braunton, it saved 85 lives. Because of the salty, wind-blown conditions, the boat-house had to be rebuilt three times until, in 1919, Appledore took delivery of a motorised lifeboat, and the last *Robert & Catherine III* was taken away, and the boat-house was dismantled. And so ended an era on the Braunton Burrows.

Another, far older, era of the Braunton Burrows reaches back into Celtic times. Once the whole estuary area that is now sand dunes is believed to have been wooded, and deer are reputed to have roamed there, which St. Brannock is said to have yoked to pull the timber to build his church.

According to an article which appeared in 1878, in the "North Devon Journal Herald", a claim is made that "some years ago the tide made considerable inroads over the sands, and the Burrows were completely flooded. This necessitated some guts being made to drain off the water. The men came across some old oak trees . . ." And, from time to time, the prehistoric remains of deer have been found there.

Along with the belief that the Burrows were once wooded, comes the intriguing legend of a lost settlement, called St Hannahs. In this town, it is said, was a chapel, dedicated to St Anne. And, up until 1860, the ruins of this ancient place of worship could still be seen, half hidden beneath the sand, standing about a foot high. The older residents of Braunton could still remember seeing evidence of cottages that had once stood alongside the chapel. They named this place "Chapel Green", and would tell you that it dated from time immemorial. No one really knows what happened to the legendary St Hannah's, although the article that appeared in the 1878 "North Devon Journal Herald", declares that it was destroyed by an earthquake – which does seem rather unlikely. But proof that people once lived there has been found, for 12th century pottery has been unearthed on the Burrows.

As for St Anne's chapel and the adjoining cottages, for years the Braunton villagers removed the limestones found there to make repairs to their own homes. Then, in 1860, a Mr Tucker, the then "warrener" removed all the stones from the ruined chapel to build himself a linhay in a nearby marsh field.

On old maps, such as the 1765 Donn, and an 1809 Ordnance Survey, the ancient chapel is clearly marked, but today its location is open to argument, for its positioning on these maps is considered by many to be incorrect.

According to Professor Hoskins in his book "Devon", the chapel once stood in the region of the old lighthouse, and was the boarding point for the ancient ferry crossing over to Appledore. Remembering that Yelland means 'old lands' (that is, Celtic settlements abandoned by Celtic tribes prior to the Saxon takeover) it is feasible to believe that St Hannah's, Appledore and Yelland were all inter-connected by ferries when the estuary was a thriving Celtic community nearly 2,000 years ago.

Back in the days when Mr William Acland (known locally as "Uncle Billy") was the Christie Estate's rabbit catcher, he was reputed to have known the site of this old chapel, and often took people to the spot. Now the only thing that remains is a font, claimed to have been found on the Burrows, and said to have belonged to St Anne's. Today, this font can be seen on the entrance steps to a small chapel on the Saunton Road, called, appropriately, St Anne's with an explanation to its origin. The story of how this font was retrieved from the Burrows is that at some time prior to 1910, it was put on a sand barge and was brought up the Pill, where it was placed in the back yard of a house in South Street. Later, a Mr S Incledon, 'inherited' this font, which he then gave to St Anne's chapel.

The Toll Road runs alongside the Great Sea Bank, ending at a square white building known today as Crow Beach House. It was built originally for the Marsh Keeper, but has been known as the White House, and the Ferry House (referring to the Appledore Ferry across the estuary). This ferry was still in operation until the beginning of the Second World War under the name of the "Pulchraffe Ferry".

From the Crow Beach House, cutting through the sand dunes, is an ancient track which links up with another old ferry way. This second track is known as the American Road, and runs into Sandy Lane. During the Second World War, the Americans widened and straightened out this old track, although they did very little to improve its surface, for it is full of pot holes.

At the Sandy Lane end of the American Road is a free car park. Near this spot is a gate which is never closed, because of the public spirited attitude of two Brauntonian men. It all started before the Second World War, when the Christie Estate placed the gate there which was kept padlocked, preventing people from using the old ferry way. In 1937 the *North Devon Journal Herald*, reported the fracas that took place.

A Mr G A Drake claimed that the gate was once more chained with the word private painted across it. Then, in the presence of a policeman, he cut the chain, and removed the word 'private'.

And, in more recent times, another public spirited Brauntonian, Thomas Slee, a master mariner, took up the cudgel on behalf of the people, for he argued that this ancient right of way had been used from ancient times by farmers, fishermen and seamen, and that the Christie Estate had no right to stop them. Every time the gate was padlocked, Thomas Slee cut the chain.

It was suggested that the farmers could each have a key, but that was not good enough for Mr Thomas Slee. Finally, in June 1976, almost 40 years later, a court ruling confirmed the right of way, and from that day everyone has been allowed free access.

Chivenor

For the people of Braunton, living near a Royal Air Force base became a fact of life to which they became accustomed. Indeed, they became so used to seeing and hearing the Hawk fighters streaking overhead, that they only became curious when an unfamiliar plane visited the Station, or the base staged its Annual Air Day. Then the locals joined the thronging crowds who flocked in their thousands to watch not only the familiar Hawks performing spectacular and thrilling displays, but all the other aircraft that 'dropped in', or flew past, as part of the day's entertainment.

This interest in the pilot's skill at flying the latest, fastest and most advanced Royal Air Force aircraft at Chivenor, dates back to its early days when it was just a small, civil airfield. Then, anything that became airborne was interesting. The North Devon Airport, as it was called, started its life as just a grassy field, which measured 300yds by 200yds. It was situated where the present day married quarters have been built, and boasted a clubhouse and a workshop.

When this airport opened in 1934, it traded under the name of The Lundy and Atlantic Coast Airline, and was run by a Mr Boyd, with two de Havilland Moths and one Dragon aircraft. Later a Monospar and a Short Scion were added. The 'airline' ran flights to Lundy, Cardiff, Plymouth, and the Channel Islands.

So that the aircraft could land on Lundy, an airstrip had to be built, although before work could begin, permission was needed from the Air Ministry. Also, the owner of the island, Mr Harman, demanded that all visitors who arrived by plane would have to obtain a permit, for which he charged a toll of one shilling. Apart from a de Havilland colliding with one of Lundy's cross walls, which meant that the wreckage had to be brought back by sea, this service proceeded in a smooth, uneventful way.

But in 1935, the local interest quickened when the first Royal Air Force aircraft flew into the airfield. It was a Hawker Hart that was making a photographic survey of Exmoor. And in the years leading up to the Second World War, the airfield became closed for civil aircraft because the Royal Air Force used it to train pilots under the Civil Air Guard Scheme.

When a war seemed inevitable, the Air Ministry cast covetous eyes in the direction of the Braunton Great Field, for this area was recognised as being vital for a coastal base for Maritime operations in the South Western Approaches. Arguments raged between the need for patriotism and conservation. Eventually, the public outcry was so loud that it

persuaded the Air Ministry to requisition, and enlarge the North Devon Airport.

It was this revamping that gave it the basic layout that can be seen today, with the air base taking its name from the tiny village on the north bank of the estuary, and the lands that included Chivenor Farm. Other places that were sacrificed to make way for the Station were Marsh Farm, and part of the Heanton Estate.

To begin with, this new Station was used only as a staging post for BOAC aircraft en route to Lisbon, but then, in December 1940, the first operational Squadron, No 252, arrived flying Blenheims and Beaufighters. From this historic moment, until the end of the war, the Station was closely associated with maritime patrol and anti-submarine operations as part of the Battle of the Atlantic. During these years, many aircraft used the Station, like the Whitleys, Wellingtons, Mosquitos, Martinets, Halifaxes, and, in 1944, a B.17 Flying Fortress.

The Station even acquired a German JU.88 when the pilot, returning from a raid over the Midlands, mistook the Bristol Channel for the English, and believed he was in France, so he landed. Needless to say, he never became airborne again. Later, the aircraft, with its new RAF markings, was used for aerial reconnaissance training by ground observers.

In 1943, a Naval Aviation Training Unit arrived, flying Seafires, the naval equivalent of the Legendary Spitfires. This was a foretaste of Chivenor's destiny, which was to become a training Station for fighter pilots.

By the end of the war, the Station was transferred to Fighter Command, and in 1947, welcomed the Spitfires. With the arrival, in 1951, of No. 229 Operational Conversion Unit equipped with Vampires and Meteors (and later the Sabres) Chivenor's role as a Station for training Fighter Pilots was firmly established until 1974 when the airfield went into "care and maintenance" after the RAF moved to Brawdy in South Wales. The 'A' Flight of No: 22 Squadron flying Search and Rescue Helicopters remained at Chivenor, much to the relief of the local people who pleaded with the MOD to "Save Our Helicopter", knowing how many lives had been saved over the years. .

In 1980 Chivenor reopened as a Hawk training station and dramatic improvements were made, but following the "Options for Change" in September 1995 the RAF moved to North Wales. But the base still had an important role to play, for on 26th October 1995 the Commando Logistic Regiment Royal Marines moved from

The impressive Hunter fighter aircraft

Plymouth to Chivenor and raised the white ensign over what had now become a Royal Marines Barracks.

Today Chivenor is a truly multi-service military bass for it is made up of Navy, Royal Marines and Army, whilst the helicopter is flown and maintained by H.Q. 22 Squadron Royal Air Force and 'A' Flight 22 Squadron Royal Air Force.

The Commando Logistic Regiment Royal Marines and 59 Independent Commando Squadron Royal Engineers are all highly trained specialists, who although primarily soldiers, some of which are the legendary Commandos, are often called upon to support disaster victims like the people of Montserrat following the violent volcanic eruptions that continued to devastate the island, and they also provided much needed protection to the Kurdish people of North Iraq when they were threatened with aggression.

The two regiments combine to make a highly-trained, quick response self-sufficient front line fighting force ready to be deployed all over the world in all manner of terrains and climates, in peace time or war, providing aid and support wherever they are needed.

Their specialist skills include setting up a fully operational field hospital in a matter of hours, clearing lanes through minefields, establishing water supplies, construction of Harrier facilities, giving logistic support on the beach during the initial stages of an amphibious landing – the list is endless, whilst the Ordnance Squadron supports the Brigade by providing ammunition, food and water; the Workshop Squadron prides itself that it can repair virtually any vehicle, and the Transport Squadron is responsible for second line vehicle and fuel carrying assets.

Chivenor Barracks is very caring of the families that are based there, providing medical care, créche facilities and parents can even have their babies baptised in a bell if they want a nautical theme to the happy event!

Over the years from 1958 the helicopter crews based at Chivenor have been scrambled over 4000 times rescuing well over 2000 civilians trapped on cliffs, cut off by the tide, or blown out to sea on inflatable lilos.

Today some missions take the crews far afield, for the base now has 3 new Sea King HAR Mk 3a helicopters fitted with the latest in satellite navigation enabling the crews to man a 24 hour coverage.

In fact down through the decades the helicopters have been so busy playing nurse-maid to the civilian population that we often forget that its primary role is supposed to be rescuing military pilots!

The Americans in Braunton

One of the most dramatic times in Braunton's history is undoubtedly the role it played when the American Army was based on the Burrows to practise for the Normandy landings. It was chosen by ETOU SA G.3 Section, because it was the only area that was large enough to accommodate regimental combat teams.

Of course as the American troops began to arrive, local people were quite unaware at the time that North Devon had been selected because it was so similar to the north west coast of France, with its vitally important tidal reaches of the Taw and Torridge estuary, and the Bristol Channel.

Once they became established at Braunton Burrows they utilised the old ferry way, which they made into the track that is known today as the American Road. They also took over 10,000 acres of farmland, and for security and safety reasons, it was necessary to move some of the villagers out of their homes, but, even then, firing had to be strictly controlled.

This American unit became known as "The Assault Training Centre", and became officially activated on 2nd April, 1943, under the command of Colonel Thompson. On September 1st, the first wave of troops arrived to start their training.

But what did the American lads think about the war and Braunton? The following, which was kindly submitted by Glenn L Kappelman who now lives in Kansas, paints a very vivid picture of how the Americans felt at the time.

The Impressions of a GI in North Devon 1944

"World War II was reaching a fever pitch when my troopship docked at Greenock, Scotland about the 9th day of June, 1944. We were on the Atlantic Ocean at the time of the D-Day landings; we all knew that soon we would be in France. But, alas, there would be that interim stay in Great Britain – a retreat that would be most appreciated as we were hearing the daily news reports of fierce fighting in Normandy.

At Greenock we boarded troop trains. The journey south provided our first view of our cousin country, England, which appeared so miniature in size and so very quaint. I can still hear the sound of the high pitched whistle as our train raced through the green countryside, past villages of stone or stucco houses and beside the manicured gardens in every backyard of the towns and cities.

We knew that we were heading for south England to be near the invasion ports. Only at Bristol were we told of our exact destination – the replacement depot camp near Barnstaple. We disembarked the train near Braunton; from there trucks carried us to the sand dunes on the North Devon shore.

The entire scene around Braunton was almost another world to a 21 year old, green soldier from the prairie state of Kansas. The vast sand dunes, the seashore, the round hills, the deep green of the fields, the stone fences and hedges, the narrow streets of the villages and the neatly manicured gardens everywhere were scenes that I had known only on picture postcards or on the movie screen. This new and different atmosphere in the seclusion and safety of Devon put me at ease as never before in my life. In fact, these impressions have remained with me to this very day.

Our arrival in Devon soon made us realize that a war was in progress. We were amazed to observe what few commodities were in the shops and what few items of any kind could be purchased. We learned what a real blackout was like. We had our first experience with censored mail. We could almost set our watches by the antisubmarine patrol airplanes returning to their base at the Braunton airfield. Too, we saw our first purple hearts which were worn by the veterans wounded in the Normandy campaign; our camp served to some extent as a convalescent center for some of the slightly wounded.

At last, in about the third week of August my turn came to board a troop train again. There was no doubt what the destination would be – this time a port of embarkation on the south coast of England and from there to a beach in Normandy. For me Devon had been a living paradox: that place so quaint with a quiet seclusion almost vacation like, was far from the real world that I had known in Kansas and in the military camps of Texas and Louisiana. Yet, now looking back forty-three years I know that Devon was the real world in 1944 and that Kansas was the never-never land to which I would someday return. Indeed, it was a sad day to depart from Braunton. It had been a safe haven for over two months when the continent was swept in flames. On the other hand we knew there would be other adventures awaiting us across the English Channel and that we must go there to finish our job.

Life on the sand dunes was very quiet but never really dull. We lived in four-man tents and slept on cots. The mess hall was a very large tent. In good weather the dining room was the sand dunes.

Basking on the beach August 1944

Glen L Kappelman on a weekend pass

Glen L Kappelman departing for Normandy

Normandy veterans wearing purple hearts July 1944

Glen L Kappelman and English friends

Shirwell Home Guard at Pilton Bridge

There were the usual GI duties of KP, guard and truck details to pick up provisions at the railhead. These truck details were sought out by the soldiers as they provided them a free "tour bus" along the beautiful, rocky coast of North Devon. Looking down on picturesque Ilfracombe would create a memory that would never fade from my mind's eye. There was plenty of time for writing letters home; there were those lazy hours on the sand just basking under the July sun. Too, there were those occasional overnight marches to bivouac areas that kept us in good physical condition. Even though the packs were heavy I did not object to these marches because they served as walking tours of the rural lanes, along the farmyards and hedges and into the fields and woods of the Devon countryside.

However, the most special event in the camp was receiving a weekend pass to Braunton or Barnstaple. There were few organized events for these brief trips. We were quite entertained just strolling through the towns or along the River Taw, taking photos or stopping at a pub to drink a "heavy" English beer.

Thanks to my camera as a means of striking up a conversation I did manage to meet a few young ladies now and then. We were generally impressed with the English girls. These encounters were always brief. Due to the continuous rotation of the GI's in and out of the camps most of us found it impossible to know the civilian population well. We found the people friendly and helpful to us. We were quite aware of their wartime burdens."

Footnote: Glenn L Kappelman moved across France as a replacement and finally joined the 106th Cavalry Group in Alsace in November, 1944 as an armoured car gunner. He served in this capacity until he saw the war's end at Wolfgangsee, Austria.

This is the American view, but what do the Braunton people remember? Apparently Nisson huts appeared, almost overnight, on the Saunton Road, just before the arrival of the troops. And they placed a Borfor (anti-aircraft?) gun on the top of the Beacon, which, from time to time, they practised firing.

There was a small internment camp to hold the people who it was believed could be a threat to National security, and some of these were put to work as farm labourers. Later, these same prisoners helped to clear the mines that had been so hastily laid at Saunton beach during the dark days when a German Invasion had appeared to be a stark reality.

The practical details of catering for the needs of this American camp must have been colossal, for apparently water was piped and pumped down to the Burrows from out of the Caen, and temporary drains were laid for them. They even took over the White House for their use.

When the Americans left, the buildings and the training areas were, with few exceptions, turned over to a Field Force Replacement Depot, and the centre became officially deactivated.

At this time many local lads, their curiosity being stronger than their caution, sneaked into what they believed to be an abandoned camp. There, they found tins of fruit and other delicacies, which had been denied them for five years, and so feeling it would be a shame to waste such pleasures, they proceeded to help themselves. Suddenly, some guards appeared, shouting and firing over the boys' heads making them flee empty handed. Once they reached the safety of their homes, they never breathed a word to anyone, just in case they received a thrashing for their exploits!

But generally, the Braunton people and their American cousins were the best of friends. And during their stay, the soliders became fascinated with the village when they learnt how old it was. They were especially intrigued with St Brannock's church. After they became friendly with the vicar, the Rev J H Prince, he was delighted when they offered to clear up the overgrown graveyard, which had become so neglected because of the labour shortage. Armed with scythes, hooks and clippers, the Americans set to work with a will. As they worked, they thought of another idea. Why not plant a tree? This they did, so that in future years the people who lived in, or visited, Braunton would know that during this period in history the two nations felt very close, for they shared the same ideals.

This was expressed at the tree planting ceremony when the US Colonel said "As this tree grows, we expect our mutual friendship to grow too."

Today this tree still flourishes, and the plaque that was placed there is a permanent reminder of the American's stay in Braunton. It reads: "This tree was planted on June 5th, 1944, by American enlisted men of diverse faiths visiting and volunteering work upon this sacred ground during the War of Liberation as a personal tribute to Britain's glorious stand against aggression".

And when the war was at last over, everybody celebrated. There were of course the street parties and the return of the loved ones back from the trenches, air fields and battle ships, with the difficult, but longed for adjustment to civilian life. But, it is VE Night that still holds the most poignant memories. There was a bonfire on the top of the Beacon, which most of the able-bodied villagers walked past in a noisy procession. My own most vivid memory was looking out of a bedroom window in South Street across to the "Mariners Arms", where airmen and other revellers were spilling out onto the street. A communal drinking vessel was being passed, from one person to another as I watched in disbelief, for it was a large, white, chamber pot!

Victory tea party in South Street

Black Horse, Church Street yesterday

The Changing Face of Braunton

Braunton's development from an isolated medieval community into the thriving village it is today took place as communications with the outside world improved.

Prior to this life was very simple; people worked on the land, and did their shopping in the market. The church was still the centre of village life, while the pubs offered somewhere to relax and gossip over a brimming tankard of ale.

Today, the two pubs that snuggle amongst the old buildings in Church Street continue to offer the villagers their 'liquid refreshment'. It is difficult to say which is the oldest, but the Black Horse with its low beamed ceiling reinforces the belief that these days people are growing taller than their predecessors. Today's landlord Mr K Dunn took over the pub in September 1999 and is relieved at being told by one of his customer's that the resident ghost quite likes him! Whilst the previous landlord confessed that this apparition lost no time in making its presence felt to him and his wife as soon as they moved into the pub. Apparently they were asleep one night when they were disturbed by the sound of heavy breathing somewhere above them, although nothing could be seen.

It is not just humans who can sense this ghost, for on one occasion their dog refused to go into one of the downstair's rooms because he was so alarmed by whatever was in there. Patrons of the pub have told Mr Carrington that sometimes the mirror in the bar can be seen swinging gently to and fro, just like it probably did when the coach and horses used to thunder along Church Street towards Silver Street in the old coaching days.

Church Street seems very popular with ghosts, and Morley Williams, who lives in one of the cottages between the two pubs, is on quite friendly terms with one departed Brauntonian, for he frequently smells his tobacco smoke in his garden, in the same way that he once did when the old gentleman was still alive.

The other pub, the New Inn, is known to have been in existence in 1525. Today on its wall hangs an amusing old advert which states: "New Inn. Church Street, Braunton. Mary Elliott, Proprietress. M.E. begs leave to return her numerous friends her sincere thanks for their kind support during the last 27 years, and trust by strick attention as business combined wtih good articles and moderate charges, to merit a continuance of the same. Well-Aired Beds, with every other accommodation for travellers. Ales and Spirits of the Finest qualtity. Commodious Stabling".

New Inn, Church Street today

The old Church Rooms, once the Braunton Museum

Opposite the Black Horse can be found a building which was home to the Braunton Museum from July 1974 until August 1997 when it moved to The Bakehouse Centre. Today's museum has enlarged its remarkable collection of old photographs and exhibits of Braunton history, and is well worth a visit, while the old Church Rooms is interesting in its own right. First mentioned in a document dated 1554 when it was still under the control of the Manor of Dean. Rectangular in shape, orginally the ground floor was partly open with pillars supporting the first floor, but was solid on the churchyard side. These pillars were at some time masoned in, but the lintels and the doorway can still be seen today. On the north end of the building, a double flight of stone steps meets at the entrance to the first floor.

Today we take our shops for granted, but in the seventeenth century produce was only available in open air markets, or the village "shambles". This was a collection or "shambles" of stalls where meat and other produce could be bought. Braunton's shambles was sited on the ground floor of the Church Rooms, with the stall holders leasing their floor space from the manor of Dean.

Later, when the idea of 'shops' (that is permanent places where wares could be displayed in a house with a front window for the public to see what was for sale) came into fashion, these market shambles became redundant. Then, cottages all along Church Street converted their front windows into shop fronts.

The Church Rooms continued to play an important part in village life once it relinquished its role as a market place, such as holding bi-annual Church Ale feasts to raise funds for the parish. It has been used as a slaughter house, and was the home of the first village fire engine. The trouble was they built the engine inside the building and then found the machine was too large to go through the door! So they had to cut part of the doorway away, and these marks can still be seen there today, visible proof of this embarrassing village blunder.

It was also an important meeting place for Braunton's officials such as the Parish Council, Marsh Commissioners and also Vestry meetings. It has been used as a store room for church valuables and processionary gear. And in 1924 a terrible row took place when the powers-that-be stopped the Parish Council from meeting there.

Up until a few years ago a Sunday School was held there, continuing the role the building has played as a place of education. It once housed a girl's school called the Beare's Charity School. But its most famous role was the part it played in the formation of the Chaloner's School.

In 1667, the Rev William Chaloner bequeathed to the parish "some land yearly value, or annuity" that could be made from the sum of £450. From this came a free school for "Children and youths" who the trustees believed deserved to learn the three 'Rs', who would otherwise receive no such education. Mr Penrose was the first master, in 1670, but other masters in later years had to first prove themselves worthy, as can be seen by the following document which states:

"To the Right Reverenant father in God, Jonathan by Divine providence Lord Bishop of Exon

We the Inhabitants of the parish of Braunton within yor Lordships Diocess, whoes names are here unto subscribed do Certifie that Mr. George Berry of our parish is very well qualified for Writing, Cyphering and teaching of Grammer and Likewise very well principled both as to Church and state to be master of our School in Braunton and therefore we humbly desire yor Lordship to grant yor License.

Witness our hands the day of December 1693.

Anthony Gregory (vic)

Southcott Luttrell
Lewis Incledon
Richard Ackland
John Symons
John Stephens
Antony Colemore
Richard Berry
Phillip Berry

In 1690, a further endowment came from an Arthur Ackland of three pieces of land at "George Yeate" (now "Goadgates"). Rents from this land were used as part of the schoolmaster's income. Also Mr Ackland left £2 a year for teaching twelve poor boys.

By 1854, a new school had been built by the Trustees, but by the mid-19th century, the founder's bequest could no longer fund the school, so it became fee paying. Today the Chaloner's School is no more, and the building has become the Fire Station.

As has been mentioned earlier, Church Street was the old 'main street' of Braunton. Right up until the 1920's it contained a grocer, butchers, tailors, smithies, drapers, bakers (including a communal bakehouse). These shop fronts on the cottages can still be clearly seen long after they have been converted back into private homes. This is especially noticeable in Nos 18 and 20. It must have been a picturesque sight back in the days when Church Street and East Street were the main shopping centres, for they were flanked with thatched buildings until slate replaced their romantic roof coverings. Old Brauntonians today love to recall some of the names of these shops – Mr Weedon the sadler, John Moon the Grocer, Howards, the Baker, Alec Reed, another grocer, Bill Simmons, Butcher, and then the Co-op. There was John's Cycle Shop, and Incledon the coal merchant. All gone now of course, for the main shopping centre is along the Exeter Road and Caen Street.

A few shops do still remain in East Street, but none survive in Church Street. The old bake house and the malt stores are merely a memory (this malt house was once the poor house and, until July 1979, when it was destroyed by a fire, became used as a warehouse).

The "Bowers" with its Tudor stone-work

Nos 24 and 24a Church Street were once a drapers, and evidence of this shop frontage can still be clearly seen today, even though it has become two separate dwelling houses.

But No 26 gives no clue to its past as a busy Coaching Inn serving passengers on their way to Ilfracombe. This was not the only place that alcohol could be obtained for there were the beer houses as well.

No 26 Church Street was once the old coaching inn

Braunton, Church Street, 1909

Church Street – 1909

Church Street – today

Up until 1898 the landlords of all the inns and beer houses made their own beer from the malt that would be obtained from the malthouse, so the standard of the drink would depend very much on the skill of a particular landlord. There was also the production of ale (the difference between ale and beer is that the latter contains hops) and was something that, according to the church records, began in 1555.

Braunton has always prided itself that when it decided to undertake a venture, it would be carried through to the best of its ability. But sometimes circumstances beyond its control conspired to thwart its best laid plans. This happened when it was decided to cut a new road through to Barnstaple. The problem was the scheduled new main road was to go through the Heanton Estate, but the Bassetts would not hear of it. Eventually, after much argument, it was decided that the road would not go through Heanton, partly because of the attitude of the Bassetts, but also because the area was marshland, and in those days they tried to avoid such land in favour of the more hilly, drier routes.

So the new road was cut along what is known today as Hills View, and then continued as the Wrafton Road, behind the Williams Arms, and there it turned left and went on up over Heanton Hill, through Heanton Punchardon and on to Barnstaple – while the Wrafton Lane passed the Manor Farm, Parson's copse, Duckpool (where you could turn up into Duckpool to reach Heanton Punchardon). In those days Chivenor Marsh, as it was called, was merely a small hamlet which contained Marsh Farm, and this is where the road ended on the edge of the marsh, coming to a dead end just short of the Bassett estate at Heanton Court.

The last shop to close in Church Street

On the Barnstaple side of the Heaton Court Barton this new road ran from the boundary of the Bassett estate towards the Strand (Ashford Strand) where it was possible to go up Strand Lane to Ashford and on into Barnstaple via the 'new main road', while the main road that is today's dual carriageway went by the Pottington Estate and over the Braunton Bridge – later to be renamed Rolle Bridge.

An account of the grand opening of this new road can be found in the Braunton Museum which reads: "May 12th, Mr Horden and several gents joined at Braunton and preceeded by the North Devon Band went in procession. An arch of laurels was erected over the bridge that was decorated with flags and bunting. Mr Horden made a speech on the occasion. The Braunton gents dined together at the Swan. About 10pm the London Mail (coach) with 6 horses drove some way down the road and back with music and banners. J W S Snow on going home nearly rode over the quay instead of over the bridge being very drunk, but was fortunately seen by Mr Gould and was prevented."

The next improvement to communications was the railway. By 1854 North Devon was linked with the national rail network with the Exeter to Barnstaple line. And with Ilfracombe rapidly developing into a popular holiday resort, attention was given to extending the railway. But there were problems. The area between Barnstaple and Ilfracombe was hilly; railway engineers viewed the possible routes. One, the eastern one, ran via Bittadon, and involved several steep hills, while the longer, cheaper, easier way went through Braunton.

But there was an unmoveable problem, the formidable Sir William Williams of Heaton Court. For ten years he stood firm, and would not entertain the idea of a railway crossing his land. But despite his opposition, the railway committee did choose the western route. So this recommendation was put to the South Western Railway.

At the same time, engineers from the Great Western Railway arrived in Ilfracombe, and announced that their Company intended to proceed with the eastern route. But still no railway was built, as the two groups argued over which was the best one to take.

Eventually the cost involved appeared to settle the matter, £160,000 for the Braunton one, and £220,000 for the eastern one. Thus convinced, the Company directors arranged for the plans to be drawn up, and attended to the details that were required for the necessary Act of Parliament. As this Act was being submitted to the House of Commons, the local people were making donations towards the railway, for they were looking forward to the freedom it would give them.

Then the shock came. The Act of Parliament had been thrown out by the Lord's Committee because Sir William Williams had convinced

them that the eastern route was a better, cheaper route.

This news so enraged the Ilfracombe people that they took the law into their own hands and rioted! And even after all this, there followed a further six years of frustration and arguments over the future railway. And always there was Sir William Williams, vowing that the railway would never go through his estate.

Eventually, in March 1870, a slightly modified version of the plans in which the route went from Barnstaple to Ilfracombe went before Parliament. This time it was accepted at every level, despite the opposition of Sir William Williams. This time he lost his case, and died a few days after the Act reached the Committee stage of Parliament.

The first sod for the railways was cut on September 27th, 1871, and on July 20th, 1874, a train at last puffed its way beteen Barnstaple and Ilfracombe, giving Braunton its longed for fast cheap form of travel, and contact with the 'outside world'.

The next major improvement was the Chaloner's Road. It marked the end of an era, removing for ever the Victorian 'Picture Book' image of the Square and its pubs which are the subject of so many old photographs.

These inns were the Ilfracombe Inn (now the Cross Tree Restaurant), The Railway Inn – known locally as Frankpitts, on the corner of Heanton Street (now the National Westminster Bank), the Barnstaple Inn (now Flair's shop), and the Red Lion (now the point where the Chaloner's Road reaches the Square and Caen Street).

The new road went from the Square, over the site of the Red Lion on the corner of Caen Street, towards Ilfracombe, severing the strips of land upon which orchards grew from the backs of the houses in Church and East Street, right down to the Caen Stream. Large portions of the Butts and Bias Lanes were sacrificed, so that today they appear as mere back allies that give no clue to their ancient purpose. But the developers must have felt some sadness for the Braunton they were despoiling, for they named the grand new bridge Butts Bridge. Further on, as the road (today's A361) continued towards Ilfracombe, it formed a junction as it ran through Church Street, leaving the old street to wend its way up over West Hills as today's Scurfield and the old Frog Lane.

But whatever their true feelings for the way that the old Square was being altered, they still looked upon the official opening of the Chaloner's Road as a grand excuse for a celebration. Out came the bunting and flags, and everyone walked along to inspect the road and stand on the new bridge.

Next, in 1931, came the Exeter Road. At the time of its construction, this grand new thoroughfare was looked upon with great

Coaches waiting to pick people up from a train

Braunton's Railway Station

Old Wrafton Station

People playing bowls close to where the railway once ran

Looking down East Street onto the end of Caen Street
Death to the old tree

wonder, for at least it would be possible to go to Barnstaple without the tedious treck of having to go all the way up over the hills, for at last the road went through the Heanton Estate.

Of course familiar places were being pulled down, like Frankpitts which stood at the corner of Heanton Street, along with the fish and chip shop that nestled under the archway. Also the old drill hall at the top of South Street. The land that was attached to the Frankpitt's pub had covered not only the site of the public house, but reached as far back as today's George Hotel's car park. So when the modern day public house was built, it retained this portion of the land, forseeing the time when it would be an asset to have such facilities.

Again several acres of orchards were felled to make way for this Exeter Road, altering forever the layout of Braunton.

While this Exeter Road was being worked upon, in the summer of 1931, Braunton suffered a disastrous flood. First there was a violent thunder storm, then a cloud burst at Spreacombe, near Georgeham, resulting in thousands of gallons of water surging down St Brannock's Hill towards Braunton. So great was the force of this flood that it ripped up roads, demolished the walls of the vicarage, and became so deep that trains and the traffic came to a halt.

As it cascaded into Caen Street, it became transformed into a frightening five foot high bore. The school children had already been hastily sent home at 12.30, so they now watched with wide-eyed wonder at the people who were looking out of their upstair's windows, for their ground floors were under 7 feet of water.

The force of this flood was so strong that an iron barrow was carried a mile from its 'moorings', and someone attempted to sail up Caen Street in a bath, before the 'keel' turned turtle, and he was forced to swim for it.

Once the Exeter Road was completed, and the use of the motor car became more widespread, it was decided that the old Cross Tree would have to be cut down. Dissenters were told it was in the way, and anyway, it was half-dead.

When its funeral came, on February 7th, 1935, people flocked to see the end of this once proud old tree. Prominent citizens, parish councillors, newspaper men, and droves of excited children gathered to watch, but everyone agreed it was a sad time, as they dug the trench around the tree's roots, and put a rope around his trunk. After all, it had stood there for three hundred years – if only it could talk!

And then, it was all over, as the big, modern tractor pulled it down. When it was on the ground, the children swarmed all over it. It was a sad end for the old Cross Tree. A slab was let into the pavement outside of the Cross Tree Restaurant, which reads: "Here stood Cross Tree 1935".

Unfortunately, this slab has not been placed on the exact spot where the tree once stood, which frequently makes amateur historians peer in puzzled fashion over old photographs of the Square, as they try to work out how the place became what it is today.

With these improvements in communications over the years came new and productive industries for Braunton. One of the most successful of these concerns was the Bulb Farm in Sandy Lane. It was the idea of a Mr Seymour Cobley, who started it with just ten acres. By 1935, it had expanded so rapidly, that during the peak of the flowering season, up to 140 men, women and boys were being employed there.

Up to thirty tons of flowers, packed in six thousand cases, were being loaded onto the Southern Railway, bound for all the major English cities. There were daffodils, tulips, iris and gladioli, and people still talk of what a wonderful sight the carpet of flowers made – quite equal to Holland.

This bulb farm continued right up until 1970, when imports from places like the Scilly Isles made their blooms uncompetitive.

The children were too young to understand the sorrow

The old Post Office
Traditional view of Braunton's Square showing the old Cross Tree and the Red Lion

The Bulb Farm workers

Another industry that old Brauntonians can still vividly remember is the Basket Factory situated in the building that is today's Clarke's Furniture, on the corner of Wrafton Road and Heanton Street. It was established by the Blackwell family in 1825, and made baskets that were sold all over the country, via the Southern Railway. Later, it was taken over by a Mr C H Martyn, who worked for the Blackwell family. He carried it on until his retirement in 1959 at the age of 69. By then polythene was fast replacing the traditional rustic baskets, so the building took over its new role of making furniture.

One feature that endured in Braunton right up to the First World War was its town crier. he was appointed annually under the old manorial system, and there are older villagers alive today who can still remember the last town crier, John Yeo Tucker. He owned a boot and shoe shop, but also fancied himself as an entertainer, although he was not very popular with the villagers, for he possessed a rather vindictive nature, which he often turned against the people of Braunton. He would organise social events, and then dress up as a harlequin, whereupon he would march around the village clanging his bell and shouting out the details of these events.

But he was greatly feared, for if he learnt any gossip, domestic upsets, or misconduct on the part of the villagers, he would gleefully relate all the intimate details to the crowd that would know under the Cross Tree, in the Square.

One thing that the Braunton people have always been ready to do is to celebrate. One of these occasions was the Silver Jubilee of George V in May 1935. Everyone took part. The streets were decorated with National flags and ships signal flags; the church bells rang before the service of thanks giving, and people lined the streets to watch the marching children, who were led by a silver band. There was maypole dancing, adult and children's sports in the park that had now been laid out between the Exeter and Wrafton Roads. And, in the evening, everyone who felt inclined went to the dance or to watch the firework display.

John Yeo Tucker, last of the Town Criers

The old Cross Tree, a draper's shop, and Frank Pitts

Standing near the Square and looking up Heanton Street

Old cottages at the end of South Street

Braunton, Red Lion Inn

Traffic found it difficult to pass through the flood

And anything that was not permanently fixed floated

But the milk supplies still got through

Old views of Cross Street

Girls of Caen Street School around 1916. The teacher was Mrs. Keffe.

Can you pick out any of your relatives? People known are:
Back row; Vera Abbot, Ethel Clark, Ivy Skinner, Emma Tucker.
Second row; ? Coats, Nora Brayley and Ruby Gould.
Front Row; Reenie Bradley, Lily Stratton, Grace Incledon, Ruth Pullen, Dolly Brey and ? Hancock.

East Street entrance to the "Agricultural"

The Mariner's Arms

Fittingly, the pages of this book feature two of the village pubs. As mentioned earlier, the "Mariner's Arms" (now known simply as the "Mariners") has always been popular with the seafaring community. Today's landlord, Mr P Payne, is very proud of the part his pub has played in Braunton's history. There are some wonderful old photographs displayed on the walls for his patrons to admire, and the huge stone fireplace still remains, claimed to burn all through the winter months.

The other pub, the "Agricultural Inn" is very popular today with not only the locals, but the tourists who pay a visit to Braunton. It has a large car park that opens out into the Chaloner's Road, which provides ample space for parking. But it was not always laid out in this fashion. Once the "Agricultural" was a hotel, and a certificate on its wall gives details of repairs that were carried out in 1929 on the main building, and also its outhouses, and a poundhouse. These poundhouses were used for crushing the apples that were grown in the hotel's orchard to make cider. In those days the main entrance to the building was in East Street, and its 'back', which is today's 'front' was a large orchard that reached right down to the river Caen – making today's pub, back to front so to speak.

Mrs Olive Berrel, a former landlady, says the pub has a ghost. Several people have sensed, or seen, its presence. A visiting medium claimed that it is a little old woman who has a shawl firmly clasped around her bent old shoulders. Mrs Berrel says that years ago an old woman who lived in the village promised to tell her the dire 'goings on' that took place in the "Agricultural Hotel", and that this was the reason that it was haunted, but she died before her tale could be told– more's the pity.

Old print of East Street

SOURCES

Chanter J F, The Church of St Brannock Braunton
Davis R, Picture Postcard Braunton
Ellacott S E, (1979) Here is Braunton Quest (Western) Publication (South Molton)
Ellacott, Braunton Ships & Seamen
Finberg H P R, The Open Field in Devonshire Studies 265-71
Hoskins R, (1954 Devon (Collins)
Slee A H, The Open Fields of Braunton – Braunton Great Field
    and Braunton Downs.
Rep Trans Devon Ass
Slee A H, Victorian Days in a Devon Village
Slee A H, Braunton Marshes. Rep Trans Devon Ass

North Devon Journal Herald, 1878 1899 1910 1935 1937
Papers from the following:
The Braunton Museum – Growth of a Village by Georgina Layland
Days of a G I By G Kappelman
North Devon Athenaeum:
Lt Col Harding papers
St Anne papers
British Museum for help on Saxon England
Braunton Library:
Braunton Parish File

. . . Photography by Tina Gaydon, Nigel Gaydon.
Permission to copy photographs was kindly granted by: The Braunton Museum,
Mrs Olive Berrel of the Agricultural Inn, Mr J H Over of the Mariners.